The Mustangs

To the Mustang Enthusiast

The Mustangs
1964-1973

A collector's guide
by Richard Langworth

MOTOR RACING PUBLICATIONS LTD
28 Devonshire Road, Chiswick, London W4 2HD, England

ISBN 0 900549 81 5
First published 1984

Photosetting by G. Donald & Company Ltd., London SW18
Printed in Great Britain by The Garden City Press Ltd.,
Letchworth, Hertfordshire SG6 1JS

Contents

Introduction and acknowledgements

Most of us reach our period of peak earnings and security in our 30s and 40s – the age at which we most often hear harried spouses say: 'The only difference between men and boys is the price of their toys'. Those of us who like cars tend to wax nostalgic for the ones we remember from our youth – not our *early* youth, when we rode around in Dad's, but our late teens and early 20s, when we perhaps drove a 'banger' and dreamed about being able to afford the latest, splendid expression of Wheeled Independence.

Although there has been a certain spillover on popular models – there are lads now driving '55 Chevys whose fathers were 10-year-olds when those cars were new – the habit of reliving our memories has been the main force in the old car movement. In the late 'Forties and 'Fifties, here in America, it was the spindly Model T and the sprightly Model A that excited car people. Toward the late 'Fifties we began to appreciate and snap up the few remaining Grand Classics: Duesenbergs, Stutzes, Marmons and multi-cylindered Cadillacs/Packards/Lincolns, and in the early 'Seventies the objects that moved us were duotoned and chromey, expressions of that period of unbridled optimism colloquially known as the Fabulous 'Fifties. Car clubs were founded more or less in keeping with these trends; the Antique Automobile Club of America came along in 1935, the Classic Car Club of America in 1953, the Milestone Car Society in 1971. It is not hard to predict that the collector movement of the 1990s will have to involve cars like the Datsun 240Z, Triumph TR6, Mazda RX7, Saab Turbo, 1984 Corvette, post-1978 Mustang, Firebird TransAm and Chevy Camaro.

The present era, of course, follows suit, and the most popular collector car – the holy grail of 15,000 enthusiasts, sustainer of its own mini-industry in original or reproduction spares, the *raison d'être* of a half-dozen fast-growing clubs and the subject of a score of books – is the 1965-73 'first generation' Ford Mustang.

Accounting for the Mustang's burgeoning popularity is scarcely difficult. It was the most popular single model in half a century. It sold over a million copies before it was on the market a year. It was, above all, an *interesting* car – available with a spectrum of options that could render it an economical six-cylinder runabout or a competitive dragster, a luxury compact with automatic transmission or a *Gran Turismo*. It was a car that transformed product thinking in Detroit, not because it was shockingly new, but because a variety of pleasant characteristics were all brought together by a brilliant car salesman, Lee Iacocca. Indeed, Iacocca's dynamic presence still adds to the Mustang's allure, for today this outspoken, hard-driving executive, a car man who really loves cars, has rescued another company (Chrysler) from sure oblivion and has made such an impression that some people would seriously like to see him run for President of the United States.

To some extent, then, the Mustang is a phenomenon greater than the 'most-popular' collector cars of the past, the two-seat Thunderbirds, the Model A Fords, the 1955-57 Chevys and the Corvettes. It is, *ipso facto*, more than just a car. It is the symbol of a generation.

To be sure, that generation does not harbour altogether pleasant memories. It saw Americans enter a war they were told they must not win, resulting in national schizophrenia symbolized by young people who sensibly asked, if it must not be won, why they were being asked to conduct it. In the Mustang's first years traditional values poured out of the national window like confetti; doubts about hitherto rockbound traditions spread so widely that even the most intrinsic symbol of America, the presidency itself, was not immune.

But people who collect early Mustangs are less interested in remembering the traumas of those years than they are the joys. And when it came to automobiles, make no mistake, the Mustang *was* a joy. An entirely new concept, it represented a revolution in America's attitude toward motoring. We had only just emerged from a period of general decadence marked by impossible styling and high-performance-but-only-in-a-straight-line. An outpouring of cars Ken Purdy described as 'a turgid river of jelly-bodied clunkers' had been produced, the symbols of which were 18-foot-long Chevrolet Impalas and Ford Galaxies. Pride of place belonged to befinned behemoths like the memorably awful 1959 Cadillac Eldorado. All this the Ford Mustang swept aside in a matter of weeks. Pre-Mustang, Americans wanted *bulk:* 'A big car that holds the road,' was the way they expressed it. They desired a dinosaur, that gulped 25¢-per-gallon petrol and was as much fun to drive as the *Queen Elizabeth.* Post-Mustang the market wanted *fun* – nippy performance plus good economy, luxurious accommodation for two, plus two extra passengers very occasionally; cars with long, low bonnets, that looked as if they were in motion when parked at the kerb.

Of course, the Mustang soon deviated from the formula it had established. By the early 'Seventies it was a much bulkier car, and its sales were disappearing; Iacocca then reverted to type with the 1974 Mustang II. But this was a car emasculated by a barrage of government regulations, and the Mustang II has never penetrated collector ranks. In 1979, Ford produced the third-generation car which, though launched after Iacocca had been sacked by Henry Ford, was nevertheless very much his automobile. The basic ideas about cars established by Iacocca's 'original ponycar' are with us yet. After a decade of wrestling with government regulations, Americans have learned how to live with them, and we are building Mustang-like cars in vast numbers again. Good ideas never die.

Since there are already enough Mustang books to comprise a good-sized library, we should probably explain why you are holding yet another. One reason is that Motor Racing Publications' *Collector's Guides,* widely recognized as the most informative studies of individual collector cars available, would be incomplete without one. An equally compelling reason is that there is a need for a book that wraps up the 'first generation' Mustang in the familiar MRP package, providing not only the history of the cars, but information about how to collect and restore them. We have therefore constructed a typical *Collector's Guide,* yet one which is unique in several respects. Significantly, it contains probably the largest series of Appendices in any book of the series. We detail the usual specifications, production figures and performance/economy tables, but we also include a section on special features and sub-models of particular collector interest – options and accessories which add considerably to the value of any given car. For the first time we produce a table of values. Not one that tells you exactly what each car and option is worth, because in the collector field this is virtually impossible – but one that gives you a working knowledge in US dollars about where you should be when you make an offer, and what the seller will expect that offer to be. As always in the collector field, the price of any individual item depends mainly on individual appreciation of the features and condition of that item. There is no set value for any set Mustang.

Because the Mustang was such a variable car, depending for its personality on a huge range of options, we have included an Appendix on the Vehicle Identification Number; where to find it, what all those figures mean, and how to interpret them. Comprehension of the VIN is essential for Mustang collectors, because some cars have been 'retrofitted' with components that were not there originally, and such cars are rightly regarded by club authorities as counterfeits. Realizing that there is a vast amount of literature around, I have also listed my own favourite Mustang books in the order that I favour them. Aside from providing a needed bibliography, these will assist the collector in further reading and research. All are available from Connoisseur Carbooks (UK) or Classic Motorbooks (USA). There is also a list of Mustang clubs, the first places to go for any prospective owner, all of which are warmly recommended.

For help on matters Mustang over eight years of writing about them I thank Lee Iacocca, the most able President any American automobile corporation has had, without whom the story, if there was any, would be much briefer. I also thank the many people within Ford who answered questions and provided quotes, who are noted individually throughout the chapters on Mustang history. Among Public Relations personnel, Bill Carroll opened up the Ford Design archives, and Don Adams, of the Henry Ford Museum and Greenfield Village, assisted me in selecting photographs. Ford Photomedia, under Bill Buffa, were – as always – of great assistance. Thanks also to Lou Weber, of *Consumer Guide,* for permission to quote from the Mustang book I wrote for him five years ago.

Collector-owned cars appearing here include Jim Northup's 1965 Mustang GT, Rick Kopec's 1966 Shelby GT-350, and Dave

Mathews' 1967 GT-350. The dust jacket photography is by my friend and colleague Bud Juneau, and we are most grateful to the owners of the three cars (see jacket flap) for their indispensible aid in setting up this lovely group photo. Some biographic notes on Lee Iacocca were quoted by permission of Michael Lamm and *Special-Interest Autos*. The competition and Shelby chapters were provided by Rick Kopec; and the chapter on collecting Mustangs, along with Appendix C, came from a Mustang expert and good friend, Gregory Wells. Thanks also to Paul McLaughlin and Jim Osborne; and to John Blunsden, Bryan Kennedy and the staff of Motor Racing Publications, who provided the opportunity for me to write this book. Finally, my gratitude must be expressed to Mustang enthusiasts worldwide for their unending enthusiasm and superb efforts in saving the cars and documenting their history.

Hopkinton, New Hampshire
October 1983

RICHARD M. LANGWORTH

A classic shape that was to win millions of admirers. The original Mustang, which was introduced as a '1964½' model, was offered with a choice of hardtop or convertible bodywork. Although a six-cylinder engine was the base power unit, the 260 and subsequent 289 cid V8s were to prove increasingly popular options and cars so fitted were identified by appropriate badging forward of the front wheels.

CHAPTER 1

Ancestors and parentage

Building a sporty car pedigree

Although proponents of the cars would have you believe otherwise, the Ford Mustang didn't simply come along and create a new species of automobile coloquially known as the 'ponycar'. What it did was bring together a variety of known marketing appeals in a tidy, inexpensive package, with a broad range of options that allowed the buyer to tailor his or her car to a rare degree – customize it, if you will, to suit the individual. As such it was a phenomenal success, and on the American collector car market today, nothing is quite so hot as the original Mustang.

By 'original' I mean the first-generation cars of 1965 through to 1973. The Mustang II of 1974 was a very successful product, but it lacked somehow the spirit and elan of its predecessor. The third-generation cars of the present are probably the best Mustangs yet, and will certainly be collectible in future years, but it is far too early to assess them in such a role now. What people care about at present, and for the foreseeable future, are their progenitors. Even 1973 may be going too far at present; but we *will* go that far herein, just to cover ourselves.

The first of the disparate factors which were brought together in the Mustang was the 'factory custom', a type of car Detroit built in wide variety after the 1939-45 war, though a concept that could be traced back to the golden age of the custom coachbuilders. Most of the latter were, of course, extinct by 1945, but that didn't prevent unusual and rather luxurious variants from emerging, wrapped around conventional underpinnings. If anything, the need for a showroom traffic-builder was greater in 1945 than in any prewar year. The American public was starving for cars, yet all that the native manufacturers could readily make available were warmed-over versions of the 1941

models; perhaps a new bit of brightwork here and there, but in essence the same old potato shapes from before Pearl Harbour. Although some independents – Hudson and Studebaker, for example – launched all-new postwar designs rapidly, the Big Three of GM, Chrysler and Ford waited until model year 1949 to produce a full line of revised models. And the Big Three, even then, accounted for some 85 per cent of domestic sales.

In 1946, Chrysler, Ford and Nash each produced 'factory customs', limited-production specials based on hold-over prewar bodies and chassis. The method in each case was to apply estate wagon-like wooden trim, using a framework of maple, white ash or yellow birch, with inserts of mahogany veneer or mahogany-like decal.

Two of these specials, the Nash Suburban and the Chrysler Town & Country, were sedans built on wheelbases of about 120in. Chrysler also offered a Town & Country convertible, built on an even longer wheelbase and equipped with an eight-cylinder engine instead of a Six. Chrysler sold over 12,000 Town & Countrys while Nash unloaded only 1,000 Suburbans, but both models served the function of drawing people into showrooms. Nash dropped the Suburban after it brought out its new postwar designs in 1949; though Chrysler retained the Town & Country during 1949-50, by 1951 the name had been applied strictly to estate wagons, and a 'personal luxury' T&C no longer existed.

The first factory specials created by the future makers of the Mustang were the Ford and Mercury Sportsman convertibles, the latter offered only in 1946-47, the former through to 1948. Production totalled about 3,500 Fords and 205 Mercurys.

The wood-decorated Mercury Sportsman, like the Ford Sportsman, was a low-volume 'factory-special' designed to attract people into the showrooms. Together, they sparked interest in the regular line of cars.

Although such figures were not impressive entries on the sales ledgers, the Sportsman exerted influence far beyond its actual volume, generating extra publicity for the rest of Ford's carryover postwar lines.

By 1949, Ford had a new design and brought forth no further Sportsman woodies, but by 1950 they were back in the factory special business again with the Custom Deluxe Crestliner and the Mercury Monterey. Each was essentially a customized version of the standard two-door saloon. The Crestliner featured a vivid duotone colour scheme and a padded vinyl top, while the Monterey offered either a padded leather or a canvas top. The idea was to simulate the look of a true convertible with its feeling of sportiness, and substitute for the pillarless 'hardtop convertible', a model which Dearborn still didn't have in its line-up. When Ford launched its Victoria hardtop in 1951 it dropped the Crestliner, but Mercury carried on with the Monterey until its own hardtop arrived for model year 1952.

By 1953, factory specials had caught on in a big way. Kaiser had its Dragon, Packard its Caribbean, General Motors a plethora of specials – the Cadillac Eldorado, Buick Skylark and Oldsmobile Fiesta. However, the purpose of these cars had since changed; now they were fielded to test public reaction to new styling and engineering ideas which might be used on future mass-production models.

By the mid-1950s, too, the sports car had finally captured America's fancy, and here entered the second broad marketing concept which would eventually result in the Mustang. Returning Yanks had brought MGs and Jaguars home from England, and their popularity fostered further offerings from Europe. The Triumph TR2, Austin-Healey 100, Alfa Romeo Giulietta and Mercedes-Benz 190SL were all designed to appeal to the American market, and all of them were successful in the United States.

American sports cars began to appear in the early 'Fifties. Following the hybrid Nash-Healey, the glassfibre-bodied Kaiser-Darrin was the first production two-seater from a major US manufacturer after the war. Its sliding doors were unique, but impractical. The car's underpinnings were based on the compact Henry J, and only 437 cars were built.

Although sports car sales were infinitesimal by US standards (they accounted for only .027 per cent of the total 1953 market), Americans were fascinated by European features like bucket seats, floor-mounted manual gear-changes and lithe, compact bodies. Public interest, small as it was, was enough to set Detroit stirring with thoughts of domestic sports cars.

Two sports models from two smaller firms had been launched by 1953; the Nash-Healey, which had made its debut in 1951, and the Kaiser-Darrin, which arrived in 1953 as a 1954 model. Another sporting entry was the very-low-volume Hudson Italia of 1954-55, a four-seat Grand Tourer based on the compact Hudson Jet. But the independents simply weren't able to produce or sell these cars in substantial quantity. They had to be more concerned with the success of higher-volume family cars, on which their profits and survival depended.

Chevrolet's Corvette, on the other hand, was a product of the most popular make in the country and the most successful corporation in the world. Powered by a mediocre Six with automatic transmission and wrapped in an unorthodox glass-fibre body complete with old-fashioned side curtains, the 1953 Corvette was really more of a boulevard tourer than a sports car. MG and Triumph fans had to put up with side curtains too – but they didn't have to

wrestle with Powerglide, or defend the car's styling. The MG T-series was classically beautiful, and the TR, though 'it looked like a shoebox somebody had put his foot through' (Tom McCahill), was at least purposeful and efficient. Yet, on the other hand, the people who admired cars like Cadillac Eldorados couldn't abide the Corvette's cramped interior and limited boot space. It was neither fish nor fowl, and at one point, around late 1954, GM very seriously considered never building another. Happily, they decided to press on. The first V8 Corvettes arrived in 1955, new styling in 1956, fuel injection in 1957, and a true sports car was born.

Meanwhile, down the road in Dearborn, Ford executives were watching the Corvette with fascination. By 1953, Ford was enjoying a remarkable comeback, engineered by Henry Ford II and Ernie Breech from the ashes of 1945. With new products and engineering, Ford had shot past Chrysler in volume during the early 'Fifties, and was planning to contest General Motors model for model across the boards. Ergo the question: Should Ford field a challenge to the Corvette?

The early Corvettes made the decision for them. 'There wasn't any question', said former Ford product planner Tom Case. 'Mr Ford wanted a civilized sports car, if we were going to build a two-

After a shaky start the Corvette was dramatically transformed into a potent sports car in 1956. This example is a factory special with duotoned hardtop (which was not offered that year) and special narrow-band whitewall tyres. The addition of a hardtop and the provision of roll-up windows made the Corvette more practical, but the car still had only two seats.

The true progenitor of the long-bonnet, short-boot ponycar was the Studebaker Hawk, which first appeared in 1956. This is a 1957 Silver Hawk V8. For a small company, Studebaker sold a considerable number of these cars, but its resources were too limited to really exploit their potential.

Ford's original two-seater, the Thunderbird, was offered from 1955 to 1957 (here is the 1957 version), but it did not achieve the sales which Robert McNamara, the company's General Manager, desired. Long after it had been withdrawn, however, Ford Division continued to be peppered with requests for its return.

seater at all. The Corvette was too spartan, too much like an MG. You just couldn't imagine Mr Ford struggling to raise one of those plastic side curtains.' Ford's response appeared in due course at the end of 1954: the Thunderbird.

This two-seater was pushed into production by the General Manager of Ford Division, Lewis B. Crusoe, who was a marketing man first and a car buff second. Thus the 1955 Thunderbird was a marketing manoeuvre, designed to outflank the Corvette by offering creature comforts as well as sporty looks and good performance. Crusoe decreed that it must have a V8 engine, and the engineers gave him the famous 292, with nearly 200 horsepower. Crusoe also demanded that automatic transmission and a lift-off hardtop be options, and he absolutely insisted that the car have conventional roll-up side windows. Handsomely if conventionally styled by Robert Maguire and Damon Woods, the 1955 T-Bird had a base price of under $3,000, and against rival Corvette it did

just what Lewis Crusoe wanted it to do. For 1955 Ford sold 16,155 T-Birds against only 675 Corvettes.

Styling for the 1956 Thunderbird was a mild facelift of the 1955 design, but the 1957 edition was extensively reworked, gaining a combined bumper-grille, tail fins and a new interior. Horsepower ratings up to 300bhp were offered. Sales in 1956 were 15,631, but they rose to 21,380 in 1957. Yet even while the two-seaters were selling briskly, Ford was planning a four-seat successor for 1958. And here we come to another milestone in the Mustang story. The decisions involved are crucial in our tale, for as Tom Case says, 'the Mustang was really the original Thunderbird revived – with two extra seats'.

When Crusoe moved up in the company hierarchy, his place at Ford Division was taken by Robert F. McNamara, later US Secretary of Defence in the Kennedy administration, and still later President of the World Bank. A no-nonsense financial man,

13

A 1960 four-seater Thunderbird with a body style which had been offered since 1958. Its greater seating capacity made it an outstanding success compared to the two-seater, but it lacked the sporting panache of the 'early Bird' and was not in the 'popular price' field.

McNamara decided that Ford Division would not build anything that couldn't be sold in great volume. Everything bearing the Ford badge must make real money. The two-seat 'Bird, McNamara rightly concluded, did not sell in high enough volume to provide a reasonable return on investment.

The effects of McNamara's policies reached beyond Ford Division and influenced even Lincoln-Mercury. A Mercury production man was brought in to alter the exclusive but money-losing Continental Mark II, the $10,000 super-luxury car which had been Ford's answer to the Cadillac Eldorados in 1956-57. Thus arrived the 1958 Continental Mark III, sharing components with standard Lincolns, and priced about $3,000 below the previous Mark II. By 1959, the Continental Division had been reabsorbed by Lincoln-Mercury, and the 1959 Mark IV was again called a *Lincoln* Continental. For the first time, also, Continental made a profit in 1958.

As for the future Thunderbird, McNamara identified three options open to his Division. They could continue the car in two-seat form as a prestige item; they could drop it out of hand; or they could remake it into a four-seater. Given McNamara's orientation to product design, it was obvious that he would choose option No 3. Simultaneously, he adamantly refused to continue the existing two-seater as a companion model, for he felt this would divert attention from the new, larger car, which needed maximum expo-

sure to stimulate initial sales.

Even before the decision was made to drop it, however, the two-seater was established as a car far different in character from the Corvette. Rather than a dual-purpose, race-and-ride sports car, the post-1955 T-Bird was strictly for the street. It looked sporty, but it handled with little more agility than an ordinary Ford saloon. It was rarely seen in competition after 1955. Its strengths on the sales floors were its sporty looks, and its invocation of unique features which followed the old 'factory special' tradition dating back to the postwar Ford Sportsman convertibles.

From a sales and profit standpoint, McNamara's decision could not be faulted. The 1958 Thunderbird was a sweeping success and – though fans of the two-seaters will deny it – it was a pretty good car in its own right. A new unit body was designed, in both hardtop and convertible guises. To make up for its added weight compared to the two-seater, the four-seat 'Bird came standard with a 352 cid, 300bhp V8. Production was around 40,000 for 1958 (when it arrived late in the model year), but by 1960 Thunderbird volume had exceeded 90,000 units. After 1963, the Thunderbird became more of a luxury car than a Grand Tourer, but it never lost the cachet of personal luxury established by the 1958 'Squarebird'. This image had strong appeal for moneyed customers who would never have been satisfied with a two-seater. It also was a saleable

The Corvair Monza, including the turbocharged Spyder variant shown here in 1962 guise with dealer-applied racing stripes, changed Detroit's thinking about compacts. Instead of spartan economy cars, thoughts turned to things like luxurious bucket-seat interiors, stick shifts, wire wheels and body stripes. The Monza's success directly influenced Lee Iacocca's thoughts for the evolving Mustang.

idea for non-moneyed customers – as Ford would soon determine.

Unlike factory specials of the past, the four-seat Thunderbird was created from the ground up specifically for its market. It was intended not only to attract people into showrooms, but to sell in quantity and make money for Ford. It met these objectives admirably, and its success was not lost on the competition.

Chrysler Corporation was soon offering bucket seats and a centre console in its high-performance 'letter series' Chrysler 300. General Motors quickly launched a squadron of 'personal' or 'performance' models from various divisions, including the 1961 Oldsmobile Starfire and the 1963 Buick Riviera. Studebaker copied the Thunderbird product package with its 1962-64 Gran Turismo Hawk, a beautiful car which had been cleverly created out of a nearly 10-year-old hardtop bodyshell by designer Brooks Stevens. Brooks admits that its roofline was precisely inspired by the 1958-60 Thunderbird. But the financial troubles that plagued Studebaker resulted in the demise of the Hawk, and shortly after-

wards the end of Studebaker cars in general.

One thing always leads to another in automotive history, and the success of cars like the Thunderbird suggested a new market segment in the early 1960s – the sporty compacts. In this area, GM was again first, with the 1960 Corvair Monza, introduced late in that model year as a trim package for Chevrolet's new rear-engine economy car. The stripped-down, lacklustre standard Corvairs had failed to sell well against the conventional Falcons, but the Monza was successful beyond even GM's projections. It is certainly the only reason why Corvairs remained in production for 10 years. It had vinyl bucket seats, full carpeting, snazzy close-coupled looks and – after 1962 – a convertible model. It was 'the poor man's Thunderbird', and as such it sold well. Priced at only $2,200 base, it cost $1,500 less than a T-Bird and about $500 less than a Triumph TR4 – yet it combined the T-Bird's four seats with the agile performance and sprightly character of the Triumph. When Chevrolet added an optional four-speed gearbox, in 1961,

15

The Mustang's only direct competitor in 1965 was the hastily concocted Plymouth Barracuda, which had appeared the year before as a fastback (some called it 'glassback') derivation of the Plymouth Valiant. Like the Mustang, it was a conventional package with front engine and rear drive, and although it was not nearly as successful as the Ford, at least Chrysler had managed to get the ponycar proportions right.

Monza sales burgeoned. The figures went from 12,000 Monzas in 1960 to 143,000 in 1961 to over 200,000 in 1962. Serious Corvair drivers chose the 150bhp turbocharged Monza Spyder, which came along in 1962 and later evolved into the 1965 Corsa. Spyders and Corsas were rapid, good handling cars of a size and character Chevrolet had never built before, and over a winding road they could give fits to MGs.

Corvair's unexpected success as a sporty compact rather than an economy car opened Detroit's eyes to a whole new and hitherto unplumbed market in the early 'Sixties. Quite naturally, the Monza wasn't alone in its field for long. By 1962, Chrysler had jumped in with bucket seat versions of the Plymouth Valiant (the Signet) and the Dodge Lancer (the GT); among larger models, the Chrysler Windsor was replaced by the 'non-letter' 300 series, which was offered with bucket seats and centre console, but not the all-out performance V8s of the 'letter' 300s. Rival GM Divisions quickly followed Monza's lead with flashy compacts like the Buick Special Skylark, Pontiac Tempest Le Mans and Oldsmobile Cutlass F-85. Even expiring Studebaker chimed in with a bucket-seated Lark Daytona in 1963, complete with the obligatory bucket seats, extra instruments, options like front disc brakes and four-speed gearbox and a performance V8 of up to 300bhp.

The hard competitors at Ford were not about to be left out of this new market. Ford's first answer to the Corvair Monza was a

General Motors' ultimate reaction to the Mustang was the Camaro, introduced in 1967 and shown here in 1968 form. Its styling expressed the contoured GM look as opposed to Ford's more angular lines. Although a fair success, the Camaro failed to head off the Mustang in the marketplace, which Ford continued to pace by a healthy distance.

lukewarm, hasty reply – the Falcon Futura coupe, which arrived in early 1961. Like the Monza, the Futura had bucket seats and a deluxe interior. A more exciting version was the Futura Sprint, offered in early 1963 as a convertible and hardtop. Sprints were powered by what would prove to be a significant engine – and a vital component in the first Mustang; the thinwall 260 cid V8 with 164 horsepower. When this light, powerful and efficient engine was coupled to an optional four-speed gearbox, the Sprint was a truly exciting car to drive.

Sprints continued in production through the first Falcon restyle of 1964 and the second restyle of 1966. By then, Ford has increased displacement of the thinwall V8 to 289 cubic inches and were offering it as a Sprint option. In 1967, the Stage 2 small-block with four-barrel carburettors brought horsepower up to 225. Mercury's Falcon-based Comet S-22 and Comet Cyclone were similar in concept to the Futura and Futura Sprint, respectively.

Yet, just as the economy models of the Corvair were not as sales-worthy as their Falcon opposite, these Ford answers to the Corvair Monza were not wholly successful replies to the popular Chevy.

Perhaps it was because the Corvair's novel rear engine and four-wheel independent suspension intrigued the kind of people who bought sporting machinery – by comparison the Futuras were flat-ordinary. In 1963 and 1964, for example, Futura and S-22 Comet production was 73,000 and 118,000, while Chevrolet produced over 350,000 Corvair Monzas in the same two-year period. If Ford was going to catch the Monza and thrive on the new market Chevy had uncovered, it would need a new and different product. That product, like the four-seat Thunderbird before it, would have to be designed precisely to cater to the market before it.

It is important for us to remember that in the years just before the launch of the Mustang, Ford was in an ideal position to create it. A succession of able managers who had joined the company since 1945 and turned Ford from an ailing giant into a mighty colossus. Ford had not only overtaken Chrysler; several times Ford cars had actually outsold Chevrolet.

The decision to launch a new, sporty and 'personal' (but by no means limited-edition) Ford occurred in 1961. But the Mustang could not have been developed without the steady sales success of the total Ford line. Had the 1961-64 models sold poorly, or had Dearborn created another Edsel, we might not have seen a Mustang until 1968 or 1969, when the ponycar craze was beginning to wane. Who can tell what it would have been like? Undoubtedly it would not have been the car that we know in the aggregate today as the first-generation Mustang. There just wouldn't have been time to evolve all its many and exciting permutations.

The reason for Ford Division's success in the early 'Sixties was largely due to its General Manager. The man who replaced Robert McNamara when he went off to join President Kennedy's cabinet was – unlike McNamara – an automobile man through and through. He combined all of McNamara's business acumen with an enthusiast's appreciation of automobile design, and the drive of a dynamic salesman. In later life, he would become almost a cult figure for millions of Americans, as he rescued an ailing Chrysler Corporation from sure bankruptcy. With a father like Lee Iacocca, the Mustang could hardly have been anything less than a stunning success.

CHAPTER 2

Defining the concept

Mustang I and the XT-Bird

Lee Iacocca's father, Nicola, emigrated to America at the age of 12 from southern Italy. As a teenager, he had scraped together enough cash to buy a secondhand Model T, which he rented out to acquaintances around his home in Allentown, Pennsylvania. Within eight years, Nicola's rental business had blossomed to 33 cars, most of them Fords, and soon he had branched out into real estate. Before the Depression, the Iacoccas had become millionaires, and through careful marshalling of their resources they managed to keep the family fortune intact through the hard times.

'Lee Iacocca never wavered from early youth in his desire to go into the auto business – with Ford', wrote *Time* in a 1964 cover story. 'For him, it was something like wanting to join the priesthood. "I suppose it was partly because my father had always been greatly interested in automobiles," he says, "and because I was influenced by family friends who were Ford dealers".'

Iacocca breezed through high school with excellent grades, received a bachelor's degree from Lehigh University and a master's degree in mechanical engineering through a scholarship to Princeton. He whizzed through an 18-month Ford marketing course in nine months, turned down an offer to become a Ford transmission engineer as too limiting, and took instead a job in a small Ford sales outpost in western Pennsylvania. He did so well here that his sales schemes were adopted by McNamara for Ford Division as a whole. This was the '$56 a month for a 1956 Ford' plan, which McNamara later said helped sell an additional 72,000 Fords that year. Promotions came thick and fast as the cigar-chomping Iacocca boosted sales of any car or truck he touched, even though Ford didn't often build them the way he would have liked.

Iacocca had the habit of keeping little black books in which he used to chart and plan his career. His black books were legendary in their own time. He once passed dozens of them out to his staff, asking each individual to write down what he or she expected to accomplish over the next few years, and in what order of importance. Then, every three months, Iacocca would grade his staff against their own self-imposed goals. When some of the older men groused about his rating method, he told them: 'Get with it. You're being observed. Guys who don't get with it don't play on the club after awhile.' At one point, he wrote in one of his own books that he intended to become a Ford Vice-President by the age of 35.

But this rigid grading system failed Iacocca himself: his 35th birthday came and went without the Vice-Presidency. 'I thought, hell, that's the end,' he later told *Newsweek*. But 18 days after his birthday Henry Ford II called Iacocca into his office and asked him if he'd accept a Vice-Presidency of Ford Division. It was probably the only time that Lee Iacocca hasn't been spot on schedule. In 1960, he took McNamara's place as Ford Division General Manager.

Another of Iacocca's black book entries was the Mustang – of course, he didn't write down that word, only an idea that sprang from his hunch that there must be a market looking for a car.

Neither did the wily General Manager reach up into the heavens and conjure up the Mustang as a vision from Olympus. His hunch was backed up by several important observations. First, people were still writing to Ford, three years after the last two-seater had been produced, begging the company to revive the original Thunderbird. Second, Chevrolet had virtually bailed out its Corvair

Ford engineer Herb Misch and designer Gene Bordinat look over the original Mustang I special and emphasize its extreme lowness. Had it been put into production a full windscreen and weather protection would have been provided.

investment by fitting some with bucket seats and calling them Monzas. Third, sales of imported sports cars like Jaguar, MG, Triumph and Austin-Healey were no longer an infinitesimal part of the US market; they were edging past 80,000 units a year, despite their generally rather high prices. Fourth, the only sporting American products – the Chevrolet Corvette and the Studebaker Avanti – were priced in very high territory, around $4,000-5,000. Could not their performance and looks be stuffed into a car selling for may be half the price? Iacocca thought it could. He wrote all this down in his little black book.

His personal experiences as a car nut were important in developing the Mustang concept. He was thinking of the kind of car he himself might want, a young man's car, good looking, fast, fun to drive, a crumpet-catcher. But his ideas were still hazy in early 1961. He had no name in mind, nor was he really committed to either two seats or four. He was not sure if he should go for a front, rear or mid-mounted engine, or a steel or glass-fibre body. Those decisions would work themselves out later. In the meantime, Iacocca had his hands full with other matters. He was trying to upgrade the rather lacklustre image Ford Division had acquired under McNamara. Though he had left the Division in excellent financial condition, McNamara's steadfast refusal to take a flyer on

an exciting idea if its sales ability wasn't guaranteed in advance had cost Ford the sporty image it had enjoyed since the first V8 back in the 1930s. His cars, *Time* said, were 'like McNamara himself, [with] rimless glasses and hair parted in the middle'.

Iacocca had arrived too late to do much about the 1961-62 Fords, but he jazzed-up the mid-year '1963½' offerings considerably. It was Iacocca who first proposed dropping a V8 into the Falcon to create the Futura Sprint; who first suggested a fastback roof on some of the big Fords; and who plunged the Division back into motorsport in a big way. With the blessing of Henry Ford II, the company re-entered NASCAR competition and was very successful on the big southern tracks. By 1965, Ford had won Sebring and Indianapolis, and had almost won Le Mans. It was obvious in those years that a new, young and vigorous hand was at the wheel.

Iacocca first broached the subject of a youth-oriented sporty car at a 1961 meeting of the Fairlane Group, an informal eight-man committee composed of top Ford executives and members of the advertising agency. The Fairlane Group was named from the Fairlane Inn Motel, on Michigan Avenue, in Dearborn, where it gathered weekly. The Group decided that Iacocca's idea should be pursued, and gave it the code name T-5. (Production 1965 Mustangs were sold in Germany under the T-5 designation.)

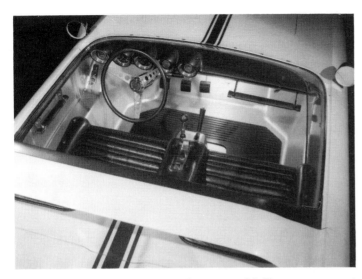

The Mustang I cockpit was spartan but purposeful. The seats were not adjustable, but the pedals could be altered to suit individual leg lengths. Most minor controls were located in a centre armrest or a side console.

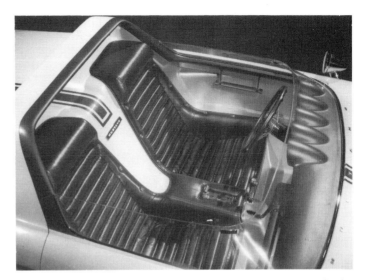

Mid-engined, the Mustang I was strictly a two-seater, and this proved to be the greatest obstacle in the way of mass production. Nevertheless, there are many who feel that it is a considerable shame that the car was not offered.

Two additional Groups now became involved; Market Research, under the direction of Ford Marketing Manager Chase Morsey Jr; and a team of young engineers and designers headed by Donald N. Frey, at that time Ford Division Product Planning Manager. The Morsey people were brought in to prove or disprove Iacocca's hunch; was the market there or wasn't it? Ford had been chary about product planning decisions since the Edsel; they weren't about to make another mistake like that. If the market *was* there, it was then up to Morsey's staff to come up with a formula for a car that would exploit it.

Here the author must fire off his traditional cannon at the folks who say we Yanks don't pick our cars, Detroit picks them for us and 'makes' us buy them. Oh no! Millions, nay billions, of dollars have been spent by the manufacturers to find out just what it is we *do* want. We asked for tail fins, and by God we got 'em; we asked for chrome, and ditto and etcetera. (More recently, it didn't take a lot of market research to know that we are now asking for quality, and Detroit, believe it or not, is making progress.) Likewise, even Lee Iacocca didn't hand us the Mustang. We asked for it. And we

got it!

It was Chase Morsey who passed our request along to the people who could meet it. After duly surveying the public, Morsey reported several interesting conclusions. First, members of the postwar baby boom were now reaching car-buying age. Second, the number of people aged 15-29 would increase by 40 per cent between 1960 and 1970, while the population in the 30-39 age bracket would actually decrease by 9 per cent. Third, more than half the projected increase in new car sales from 1960 through to 1970 would come from buyers between 18 and 34 years of age. Fourth, car styling in the 1960s would have to reflect the preferences of this new group of young buyers, not the old fogies who had gained their thrills from tail fins. (Morsey's report concluded, '...36 per cent of all persons under 25 liked the "four on the floor" feature. Among those over 25, only 9 per cent wanted to shift gears. Bucket seats were a favourite feature among 35 per cent of young people, as against 13 per cent in the older groups. Fifth, buyers were now more educated, more sophisticated and more willing to spend cash for what Morsey viewed as 'image extensions'.

Sixth, more families had money. The number of families with incomes of $10,000-plus was expected to rise 156 per cent between 1960 and 1975. Thus more families would be able to afford second, third, even fourth cars. Women and teenagers especially were the family members who would dominate the choices of these second-string automobiles.

The answer to Iacocca's poser, then, was: Yes; a sizeable market for a youthful, sporty car *did* exist. It was big enough to create a substantial demand for the right product – distinctive, sporty, but not too expensive. The question now was: What exactly should this product be? Ford set out to build some proposals in order to further their considerations.

One of the first alternatives considered was the Mustang I, a two-seat sports car directly reviving the original Thunderbird concept. Aimed more at the Triumph-MG market rather than the Corvette-Jaguar field, such a car might be the market-filler Morsey had identified. The Mustang I is now quite a famous predecessor to the production cars, and it lives on at the Henry Ford Museum in Dearborn. It is worth discussing, in order to illustrate what the production Mustang *wasn't*.

The Mustang I was engineered by Herb Misch, formerly of Studebaker-Packard; styled by Gene Bordinat, longtime Ford designer and head of Ford Design today; and product-planned by Roy Lunn, formerly of Aston Martin, later a member of the Ford Product Study Vehicles Department. Lunn laid out the Mustang I's design goals.

As a challenger to Triumph and MG, the car was planned for a wheelbase of 85-90in and an engine of 1½ to 2 litres, mounted centrally in a multi-tubular frame covered by an aluminium body. Since it was impossible to build a prototype body rapidly in Detroit, Ford contacted Trautman and Barnes of Los Angeles, who fabricated the frame out of 1in steel tubing and the stressed-skin body from .06in thick aluminium panels. An integral rollbar/seat structure gave the thin body rigidity, but this in turn required a fixed seat – so adjustment was provided for the pedals and steering wheel. The pedals were mounted on a sliding box-member, which allowed their position to be altered to suit any driver.

Lunn and Misch designed the four-wheel independent suspension, an innovation for Detroit. The rear suspension used upper wishbones and lower triangulated arms coupled to radius rods, with attachment points widely spaced to distribute stress evenly throughout the car's structure. Up front were wishbones, splayed coil springs and Monroe telescopic shock absorbers. All shocks and springs were adjustable for ride height and firmness. Steering was by rack-and-pinion, a unit similar to that used for the Ford Cardinal prototype, which later evolved into the German Taunus 12M. The steering was geared to provide 2.9 turns lock-to-lock and a turning circle of 30ft.

The engine was placed behind the cockpit, ahead of the rear wheels. Derived from the Cardinal, it was a 60-degree V4 displacing 1,927cc (90 x 60mm), producing 90bhp at 6,500rpm and breathing through a single-throat Solex carburettor. A competition version of this engine had two twin-throat side draught Webers and a crossover manifold, and produced over 100bhp. Bolted to the powerplant was a four-speed transaxle, also Cardinal-derived, with a cable-operated gear-change. A 7½in diameter clutch with special linings, adapted from the English Ford Consul, was used. The transmission ratios weren't very close (4.02, 2.53, 1.48 and 1.00), but the 3.30:1 rear axle ratio made them suitable for the V4 engine.

The Mustang I followed accepted sports car practice in having disc brakes at the front and drums at the rear. The parking brake operated on the rear drums – also standard practice in built-to-a-price sports cars. The front discs were 9½in Girlings taken from the English Ford 109E. The 13in magnesium-alloy wheels were provided by Lotus, and they were shod with Pirelli radials.

This prototype Mustang had a 90in wheelbase, 48/49in front/rear track and measured 154in overall. It was very low, and its lightweight construction gave it a kerb weight of merely 1,200lb, making up for any power deficiencies in the V4 engine. Its top speed was about 115mph. It was also quite slippery by aerodynamic standards of the day. There was no room for a conventional radiator up front, so two diagonally mounted radiators were fitted, each equipped with a thermostatically controlled fan. The spare tyre was stored in the front compartment and the 13-gallon (US) petrol tank had a quick-fill neck.

Mustang I styling went from sketch to approved clay model in just 21 days under the direction of Gene Bordinat, and Roy Lunn assured that the form would meet FIA and SCCA regulations for competition. The rollbar and racing windscreen were SCCA-approved, though a conventional windscreen was contemplated for volume-produced models. No top was designed, this being left

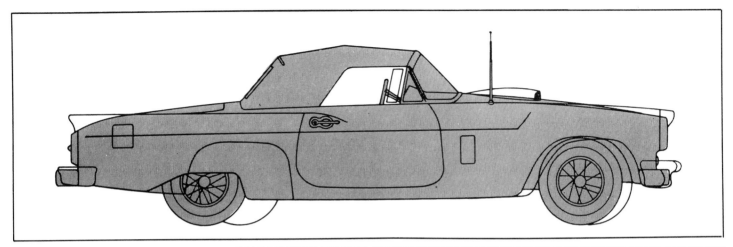

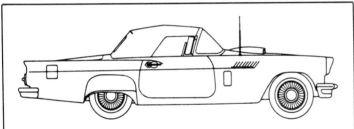
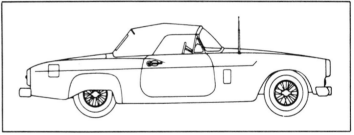

The Budd Body Company, a longtime Ford supplier, offered this proposal for an XT-Bird utilizing the chassis and running gear of the 1961 Falcon and a modified version of the 1957 Thunderbird two-seater body. The upper drawing shows the proposed XT-Bird in the shaded area with the outline of the 1957 Thunderbird superimposed. A comparison of the earlier Thunderbird and the proposed XT-Bird is offered by the two lower drawings. Budd had retained the Thunderbird dies and proposed to use many of them for the XT-Bird.

to detail engineering should the design be approved for production. (The engineers had conceived of a folding hardtop, which would have been a unique feature.)

Interior styling was rushed, but nicely executed. The instrument panel offered five pods to house the fuel gauge, speedometer, rev-counter, ammeter and water temperature gauges. Ignition and light switches were mounted in the driver's armrest, the choke and horn button in the centre console alongside the gear-shift and handbrake levers. A small rubber mat covered the central floor. The cockpit was stark, but eminently functional and in keeping with the design goal of low production costs.

The Mustang I was displayed to the public at the US Grand Prix at Watkins Glen in October 1962, where it was driven pre-race around the circuit by Dan Gurney. *Car and Driver* borrowed it for a road test, clocked 0-60mph times in the 10-second range and fuel economy around 30mph (US). 'It reminds us of the first two-seat 1,100cc Coventry Climax-engined Cooper', the editors wrote, '[but] more forgiving. It can be braked well into a turn, and with power on its stability is striking.' The magazine did suggest that more luggage space was needed, and the retractable lights would require electric servos; on the prototype, they had to be hand-cranked into position.

While the Mustang I excited sports car fans to a frenzy, this ironically proved its undoing. Iacocca, who was carefully charting the reaction, recalls: 'All the buffs said: "Hey, what a car! It'll be the best car ever built." But when I looked at the guys saying it – the offbeat crowd, the real buffs – I said: "That's sure not the car we want to build, because it can't be a volume car. It's too far out".'

Similar drawbacks attended a second proposal which drew some attention at this time, the Falcon-based XT-Bird. This car was an exercise in production engineering by Budd, long-time supplier to Ford, and not precisely a Dearborn project. Budd, which had tooled the bodies for the original two-seat Thunderbird, still had those dies in 1961. Budd concluded that this tooling might be economically updated for a new production car combining the chassis and drivetrain of the 1961 Falcon with a modified 1957 Thunderbird body.

Removing the Falcon body from its chassis but retaining the floor structure, Budd attached a 'modernized' 1957 T-Bird body, shorn of its tail fins and with lower front fenders. Ingeniously, they managed to retain the 1957 Thunderbird dashboard and cowl, which remained perfectly modern. But they did eliminate the severely wrapped windscreen and 'dog-leg' A-pillar of the T-Bird, and revised the quarter-lights. The XT-Bird had a folding soft top, which disappeared into a well ahead of the deck lid, not unlike the old two-seater. There was also a rear jump-seat, which could be folded down to form a luggage platform. Budd proposed a steel body and estimated that the finished production car could retail for $2,800 base price.

Budd executives prepared an elaborate folder for Ford executives, hoping to interest the Fairlane Group in this car to fit the newly defined sporty-compact market. They pointed out that two-seat Thunderbirds were already selling for their original list prices and more; this, Budd suggested, proved that there was a strong demand for an updated two-seater. 'The total tool, jig and fixture costs for production of the XT-Bird would not exceed $1.5 million', Budd wrote. 'We could ship the entire body-in-white for the XT-Bird to the Ford Motor Company for a total unit cost of between $350 and $400... We believe that we could be shipping complete bodies-in-white for this car six months from the day you authorize us to start the job.'

No authorization came. Lack of full four-passenger capacity was the XT-Bird's main limitation, for Iacocca had just about decided that the new product should be a genuine four-seater. But its rather dumpy lines didn't set many hearts pounding, either. Besides, Ford's own styling studio had far better ideas to offer than a warmed-over two-seater, and by the time Budd made its approach there were hundreds of proposals kicking around at Styling. It remained only for Iacocca and Company to pick the right one. They did.

CHAPTER 3

The ponycar takes shape

Mustang II and the Oros influence

While the Fairlane Group was looking at and turning down the Mustang I and the XT-Bird, Ford Division Advanced Styling had proposed an open racing car called Median and a two-seat sports car called Mina. Neither of these fitted the proposed concept either – they were fringe models, not volume cars. Finally, the Fairlane Group asked for a single proposal, a four-seater they called the 'median sports car', to be worked up in coupe and convertible body styles. It captured the personal flavour of the two-seat Thunderbird, yet it offered full four-seat capacity. (Medians with jump seats and two-place-only seating were also offered, but rejected.)

The median sports car led to a second generation of styling studies under the generic name Avventura. There were 12 different clay models in the Avventura series, one of which became the Allegro X-car, first shown publicly in August 1963. There were over a dozen variations of this model, each differing slightly in dimensions and interior packaging.

The Allegro was built on a 99in wheelbase, stood 50in high (10in higher than the Mustang I!), was 63½in wide and 170in long. Its powerplant was the 144 cid Falcon Six, front-mounted with manual gearbox, with a conventional live rear axle located by leaf springs. The cost analysis people were making their opinions felt by now, and Ford was leaning towards a more conventional package, borrowing many off-the-shelf components. Designers stated that the Allegro could accommodate the Falcon Sixes or the Taunus V4s with their front-wheel drive, but Ford Division leaned towards Falcon technology with its conventional front-engine/rear-drive componentry.

Like the Mustang I, the Allegro's seats were fixed and the pedals adjustable fore and aft. The steering wheel was adjustable up and down, and also swung out of the way like that of contemporary Thunderbirds. A 'memory button' allowed the wheel to return to a preset position once the driver was seated. The Allegro also featured retractable seat belts, then a novel idea; the belts were anchored to the seats which, being fixed, were capable of supporting them. Studying and narrowing down the many Allegro variations occupied Ford Division for about a year, until mid-summer 1962. It never seemed quite right, however, and at that time Iacocca, his design team, and Henry Ford II decided to start over with a whole new series of clay models.

This time they were able to present the designers with a definite set of specifications: a 2,500lb kerb weight; a 180in maximum length; four bucket seats; a centre console to house the gear lever; and a target base price of $2,500. The latter virtually guaranteed massive use of production mechanical components, mostly Falcon. But the designers were left an 'out' – they could create a very long list of optional extras which would allow the buyer to tailor each car for economy, luxury, performance, or various combinations of these. This long option list was yet another milestone in the story of the Mustang's creation. It was probably the single most important factor behind the car's early success.

Four styling studios were asked to work on the new series of proposals: Lincoln-Mercury, Corporate Projects, Ford Division and Ford Motor Company Advanced Design. All reported to Bordinat, who had given them just two weeks to come up with suitable scale clays. Seven clay models were produced and arranged side-by-side at the Ford Design Center courtyard. Of the seven, one leaped out from the pack. 'It was the only one in the courtyard that seemed to be moving', Iacocca said. Henry Ford II agreed.

The 99in wheelbase Allegro prototypes were built to a prearranged size and specification using the Falcon 170 cid six-cylinder engine and a conventional drivetrain. Note the Thunderbird influence, also the Corvette being used for comparison in the background.

Frontal view of the Stiletto, a T-bird-like clay model in the Allegro series featuring a simple horizontal bar grille treatment between single headlamps.

This proposal was created by the Ford Division studio under Joe Oros, who would later become Executive Director of Ford and Lincoln-Mercury design. Members of Oros' team included Gail Halderman (Studio Manager) and David Ash (Executive Designer). The Oros group had gathered to talk about the assignment before anyone put pencil to paper. 'We said what we would and wouldn't do', Oros recalled. 'We didn't want the car to look like any other car. It had to be unique.'

They talked so much that, once they started, the drawing took only three days. In final form, the styling looked very much like the eventual production Mustang, but without a front bumper. Oros called it the Cougar, though the name was later changed to Torino, and the variation Turino. Finally – and confusingly – the prototype was labelled Mustang II. Oros deliberately painted the clay model white, so it would stand out at the showing and increase his team's chances of winning this not-so-friendly intramural styling contest. Judging by the reactions of HF2 and Iacocca, he succeeded handily.

The Cougar/Torino/Mustang II was based, like Budd's XT-Bird, on the Falcon floorpan. To provide genuine four-passenger

We should be thankful that the wilder suggestions which were offered in connection with the Allegro series of studies were quietly ignored, or at least forgotten. There was a hint of German Ford Taunus about the headlamp treatment.

This Allegro proposal from the Lincoln-Mercury studio shows a choice of taillamp treatments and a flat rear screen in conjunction with tapering rear fins of different configurations. Note the twin exhausts emerging from the bodywork.

seating capacity, it used a wheelbase of 108in, only 1½in shorter than the production Falcon. The track was 56in front/rear and the overall length 186.6in – a hair over the specified maximum. Oros made sure that the car would accept Ford drivetrains up to and including the 289 cid V8 and four-speed all-synchromesh transmission.

At Watkins Glen, in 1963, Ford displayed a running version of the Oros car, also called Mustang II. Those who saw it considered it just another dry run, like the Mustang I had been – some of them were disappointed that the Mustang I was never produced. Actually, it was as close a preview to the forthcoming production car as anyone would see. Iacocca hinted broadly that production was now seriously intended. 'Our preliminary studies indicate that a car of this type could be built in this country to sell at a price of under $3,000', he told the press.

Car enthusiasts exist at Ford-USA, although it isn't always obvious, and Joe Oros was a car enthusiast. As such, he would have liked to build a two-seater, at least as a companion model. By late 1963, he was showing one, the Cougar II, with dimensions quite close to the AC Cobra: 90in wheelbase, 50/52in track, 48in height and 168in length. The Cougar II was a running prototype powered by a 260 cid Fairlane V8 with four-speed gearbox and independent suspension all-round. 'The aerodynamics look reasonably good and the performance should be excellent', said *Road & Track*, 'especially with one of the hotter versions of the Cobra-ized Fairlane V8.'

The Cougar II was certainly the nearest thing to a genuine street sports car turned out by Ford in this period. It also had the smoothest styling of any of the Mustang prototypes. But it suffered the same deficiency as all the two-seaters before it – it could not command a high enough volume to assure a significant return on its high tooling cost. Neither did it fit Iacocca's idea for a four-passenger car. And perhaps it looked a bit too much like the Corvette Sting Ray, which was anathema at Ford.

On September 10, 1962, Oros' original four-seat proposal was 'validated' for production engineering. At this point, Ford Engineering got formally involved. This was unusual, because the engineers were usually called in at a much earlier stage in any car's development. The need to keep styling options open was probably the cause of the delay.

Jack Prendergast, Executive Engineer for Light Vehicles, said: 'Styling kept the engineers out too long, but even so Engineering and Styling worked together very smoothly.' Except for the routine compromises needed to modify a styling prototype for mass production (conventional bumpers, round headlamps, a less rakish windscreen angle), relatively few changes were made to the Oros design. Engineering went out of its way to keep the car intact. This is a rare thing in Detroit, and it worked to the Mustang's advantage.

Because the chassis, drivetrain and lower structural components were all off-the-shelf, the largest task Engineering faced was the

A more conventional approach in the Allegro series, in line with the larger Ford passenger cars of the period.

One concept that the Allegro exercise established was the long-bonnet, short-boot shape, as demonstrated here by a late prototype. The competitive comparison cars in the background are a Pontiac Tempest Le Mans and a Corvair Monza.

As a follow-up to the Allegro exercise, four Ford styling groups were given the task of preparing various new shapes, a typical example being this Ford Styling entry, which bore a very close resemblance to the production Thunderbird of the time, especially at the rear. The neat grille pattern was to become familiar on certain European Fords in the years ahead.

Mustang's body. Its original length had been trimmed now to 181.6in, identical to the 1964 Falcon and close to the original specification of 180in. Why wasn't the wheelbase identical? (It would have saved some money.) 'Because', said Ford Division, 'we didn't want to share any sheet metal with the Falcon.' To this extent, the Mustang was to be an all-new car.

It wasn't as easy as it appeared, however. 'We had to bend something like 78 Ford Motor Company in-house standards or rules in order to build this car', said Gail Halderman, Manager of the Ford Styling Studio. For example, the rules prohibited radical tuck-

under of fenders, minimal bumper to sheet metal clearance, die-cast bezels in front of the headlamps. The production car featured extreme tuck-under fore and aft, tiny clearances between body and bumpers, and die-cast bezels galore. Neither did the engineers tinker with the stylists' design ideas, except where they couldn't make the car fit together without modification.

The vast variety of optional engines and horsepower ratings required a rigid base capable of handling them all. Prendergast: 'The platform-type frame, evolved from previous light-car experience, was designed to be really in the middle. All the various chas-

It was soon obvious that Ford Division stylist Joe Oros had the legs of his intramural competitors with the Torino, *née* Cougar, which benefited from a wide track and a 108in wheelbase. Smooth and handsome, the Torino lacked most of the styling excrescences of other proposals, and Lee Iacocca and Henry Ford II agreed that it should be the basis of the production car to come.

From the original Torino/Cougar came a running prototype named Mustang II; like the Mustang I it was widely shown throughout the country and was on display at the 1963 US Grand Prix. It was the direct progenitor of the production Mustang, which adopted most of its styling features.

31

The triple rows of taillamps were one of the distinguishing features of the Mustang II which were carried through to the production car, but the quad exhausts were quietly forgotten, at least for a while.

Nearing production, the Oros design was rendered practical for street use with bumpers front and rear. This is a very late production prototype, still bereft of name plates, and Ford photographic records indicate that at this stage the car was still being called a Cougar.

sis components were attached to the underside, and all the body components were installed topside.' Heavy box-section side rails with five welded-in crossmembers formed the base. The convertible used heavier-gauge steel and extra reinforcements in the rocker areas. The frames of the first coupes were so stiff they actually resonated vibrations. Accordingly, the coupe chassis was softened. Prendergast pointed out that during the Mustang's preparation, Engineering had learned a lot about noise, vibration and harshness through experience with the compact Falcon. Thus the choice of such components as suspension members was easier and more sound than on earlier small Fords. The Mustang's suspension, in fact, drew heavily on components from the later Falcon Sprint and Fairlane series cars. Indeed, the latter were actually modified in production to anticipate the need for sharing components with the Mustang: to accommodate Mustang's low bonnet, engineers lowered the air cleaner and countersunk the radiator filler cap on all Falcons and Fairlanes in mid-production during late 1963, allowing the Mustang to use these bits unmodified. In a similar way, all mechanical parts for the Mustang were in production and catalogued several months before the actual production car made its debut.

One of the final contretemps surrounded the actual name of the

The Mustang virtually as the public would see it on announcement day, April 17, 1964. However, this styling mockup still has to receive a crossbar on the grille and the dated numberplate is misleading as all production Mustangs were technically 1965 models, although occasionally referred to in the early days as '1964½s'.

new car. Although the name 'Mustang' had been seriously considered very early, witness the first Mustang I two-seater, it took many months before this designation prevailed. Various Ford departments had applied different titles to the prototypes, including Allegro, Avventura, Cougar, Turino/Torino. Henry Ford II favoured 'T-Bird II or Thunderbird II. Surprisingly, Lee Iacocca had no strong preferences.

John Conley, of Ford's advertising agency, went to the Detroit Public Library in search of names. (Conley had previously come up with Falcon for the Ford compact, though after it was chosen Ford learned that it would have to obtain the rights from Chrysler,

which had used it on a 1955 sports car prototype.) Instead of considering birds, Conley now searched through names of horses. Along with Mustang, he considered colt, bronco, pinto and maverick, all four of which were eventually used by somebody – Colt by Dodge/Mitsubishi, Bronco/Pinto/Maverick by Ford. Conley concluded, though, that Mustang was the best possible name. It connoted cowboys, prairies, the romantic West. It was easy to spell and to remember. As one Ford ad man said: 'It had the excitement of the wide-open spaces, and it was American as all hell.' A symbol for the wild, free-spirited horse of the Western plains was thus carved out of mahogany for the original die-casting of the now-familiar emblem that graced the production prototypes.

Target date for the Mustang's introduction was April 17, 1964. It would be called, informally, a '1964½' model, but all of the first group of cars were properly 1965s. The location was the New York World's Fair, which opened the same day.

Of course, the public appetite had been whetted for years by a succession of sporty Ford showcars, beginning with the Mustang I. But Ford decided to whet it some more by 'accidentally' disclosing the Mustang in advance of the formal announcement. On March 11, HF2's 20-year-old nephew, Walter Buhl Ford III, duly paraded a black pre-production Mustang convertible to lunch in downtown Detroit 'without official authorization'. The first newspaper man to spot it was Fred Olmsted, Auto Editor for the *Detroit Free Press*. Olmsted called a photographer, who hurried over and snapped it. The photo was picked up by *Newsweek* and other national publications, giving a huge audience a peek at the Mustang-to-come. It was a beautifully orchestrated piece of PR in which Ford played the injured and compromised party while the dealers carefully took down the names and addresses of all the prospects who called to find out when they might buy one.

About the only people disappointed with such tactics were the editors of *Time*, who thought they'd made a deal for exclusive photo coverage of the Mustang as it was being developed. *Time* photographer Ed Bailey had been with Oros and Bordinat almost since the beginning of the Mustang II project, and *Time* had agreed not to publish anything until formal introduction. *Time* kept its side of the bargain, but Ford didn't, and *Life, Look, Esquire, US News* and *The Wall Street Journal* all broke with Mustang stories before *Time*. On the evening of April 16, Ford bought the 9pm time slot on all three major TV networks, and an estimated 29 million people saw the Mustang's unveiling without leaving their lounges. The next morning, 2,600 major dailies carried announcement ads and articles.

Ford invited about 150 motoring writers to the World's Fair preview, where they were wined, dined and set loose the next day with a herd of cars to drive from New York to Detroit. 'These were virtually hand-built cars, and anything could have happened', recalled one Ford press officer. 'Some of the reporters hot-dogged these cars the whole way, and we were just praying they wouldn't crash or fall apart. Luckily, everyone made it. But it was pure luck.' The luck paid off in glowing reports during the following weeks and months.

Mustangs were soon being displayed in airport terminals, hotel lobbies and dealer showrooms, boldly accompanied by big signs listing their even-then incredible base price: $2,368 fob Detroit for the coupe model. The reaction was instantaneous and tremendous. One San Francisco trucker stared so hard at a Mustang in a dealer showroom that he drove right through the plate glass. A Chicago dealer resorted to locking his doors – a most un-dealer-like gesture – to keep the crowd at bay. A Pittsburgh dealer made the mistake of hoisting his first and only Mustang on a lube rack. The crowds pressed in so thick that he couldn't get it down until supper time. At one eastern dealership, where 15 customers wanted to buy the same new Mustang, the car was auctioned off – but the winner insisted on sleeping in it to be sure it wasn't sold out from under him before his cheque cleared the next morning. Iacocca's hunch had been right all along!

The only problem Ford had with the Mustang was that production couldn't meet demand. All the early deliveries were sold for handsome amounts well above retail. Long before the introduction of the car Ford had projected first-year sales of 100,000 units; just before debut, Iacocca raised the figure to 240,000 and switched over the San Jose, California, plant to Mustang assembly. But it took only four months to sell 100,000 and seven months to peddle 250,000, and during the 1965 model year (April 1964 through to December 1965) an unbelievable total of 680,992 cars were sold. This figure was an all-time industry record for first-year sales and the millionth Mustang had been assembled by March 1966. The sales record is the more impressive in view of the limited body styles available – only coupe and convertible until September 1964, when a fastback was added.

A legend had been created overnight. But if the Mustang was an instant hit, it was so because years of planning and dedication had been put into its concept and execution. As a sports car it was certainly deficient in some ways; but as a sporty car it was better than anyone had expected. And it was the start of the ponycar revolution in Detroit.

CHAPTER 4

Mustangs 1965 to 1966

Hardtop, convertible and fastback

The bulk of interest in Mustangs still hovers around the first two model years. It has been hovering a long time – partly because there is still a very good supply of these cars, and partly because they were the quintessential Mustangs, the real thing, the grand original. From 1967, changes started to be made that weren't always for the better, as later chapters will record. Thus it behoves us to make a thorough study of the first two model years. For the potential Mustang collector, there is no substitute for information.

There really was no such thing as a typical Mustang, which accounts for its schizophrenic reputation among collectors today. The Milestone Car Society, which has thus far failed to certify any save Shelby versions as Milestone cars, has been under fire of late to add more Mustangs to its list of 'great cars of 1945-1967'. MCS' standard retort is the question: 'What is a Mustang?' and MCS officers point out that it is at once an economy bucket with six cylinders and a fire-breathing Grand Tourer. They are right, but they are also thinking about nominating the latter *type* of Mustang – in answer to popular demand.

It was the broad option list of the original Mustang which made it so appealing, of course, and detailing that list is necessary here, if difficult. Somebody once calculated that you could, by judicious use of the option list, produce the first year's worth of Mustangs without ever repeating yourself, which illustrated the magnitude of the variety available.

Standard equipment on the original cars was the 170 cid Falcon Six, a three-speed manual floor-shift transmission, full wheel covers, padded dash, bucket seats and carpeting. Typical options to this basic spec included Cruise-O-Matic transmission or four-speed or three-speed with overdrive; three flavours of V8 engine;

limited-slip differential; Rally-Pac (tachometer and clock, mounted atop the steering column); special handling package; power brakes (or, from late 1965, power discs); power steering, air conditioning; centre console, deluxe steering wheel; vinyl roof covering; pushbutton radio with antenna; knock-off style wheel covers; 14in styled steel wheels; whitewall tyres. There were also a number of option packages. The Visibility Group included outside rear-view mirrors; the Accent Group offered pinstriping and rocker panel mouldings; the Instrument Group consisted of needle gauges for fuel, water, oil pressure and amperes, grouped around a circular (instead of a horizontal Falcon-type) speedometer; the GT Group included disc brakes, driving lights and special trim. The most expensive option – air conditioning – cost only $283. Many of the sporty extras, like the handling package ($31), front disc brakes ($58), Instrument Group ($109) and Rally-Pac ($71) were easily affordable. So for less than $3,000, or about £1,000 at that time, you could 'build your own' Mustang. All you had to do was wait for it to be delivered.

The basic character of each car started with its engine, of course, and during the 20-month 1965 model run powerplant offerings were shuffled slightly. The original standard 170 cid Six with 101bhp was dropped after September 1964 (which is considered the 'break' between the '1964½' cars and the 1965s. It was replaced by a 200 cid Six with 120bhp, a higher compression, redesigned valving and seven instead of five main bearings. The 200 also had an automatic choke, short-stroke cylinder block design for longer piston and cylinder wear, hydraulic lifters and an intake manifold integral with the cylinder head.

The smallest Mustang V8 among early models was the 260 cid

Although base Mustangs were powered by the six-cylinder Falcon engine, the 260 cid small-block V8, as fitted to this car (identified by the badge on the front wing), was available for a modest $108 extra.

A third body style, the 2+2 fastback, was added to the Mustang line in the autumn of 1964. This is the base six-cylinder version, which accounted for a small minority of the 77,000 1965 fastbacks produced.

thinwall with 164bhp. Derived from this was a 289 V8 with 195bhp via a two-barrel carburettor or 210bhp with the four-barrel. A Hi-Performance 289 had 271bhp. After September 1964, the 260 was discontinued and the two-barrel 289 with 200bhp became the base V8. At the same time, the four-barrel was boosted to 225bhp; the 271 was left unchanged. While the four-barrel 225 engine cost only $162 extra, it took $442 to buy the 271 version.

This was a classic American engine, one of the best in its field – light, efficient, powerful and capable of extremes of modification. Thinwall casting made it the lightest cast-iron V8 on the market. Short-stroke design, full-length/full-circle water jackets, high-turbulence wedge-shaped combustion chambers, hydraulic lifters, automatic choke and centrifugal vacuum advance were all part of the specification. The four-barrel units achieved their higher bhp by increased carburettor air velocity matched to the performance curve of the engine. They also had different valve timing and a higher compression ratio, and they required higher octane fuel.

The Hi-Performance 271, the ultimate Mustang powerplant, developed nearly one bhp per cubic inch and 312lb/ft of torque at 3,400rpm. It had a high-compression cylinder head, high-lift cam,

During 1965 Ford introduced a GT option pack, which included disc front brakes and a different brake pedal incorporating the lettering 'DISC BRAKE' in a roundel as a reminder to the driver. Revised instrumentation with a central speedometer was another GT feature.

Coincident with the introduction of the fastback, Ford changed the Mustang's V8 option from the 260 to the 289 cid engine. In standard form, with two-barrel carburettor, 200bhp was offered, but 225bhp (four-barrel) and 271bhp (Hi-Performance) versions were also available.

Three looks beneath the bonnet, or hood, of 1965 V8 Mustangs. From its introduction as an option in the autumn of 1964 the 289 cid engines in their three guises became synonymous with the Mustang's continuing success story. Identification of the Hi-Performance version by its chromed air cleaner is not always reliable as many a lower-powered 289 has been visually modified in this respect. The car's original engine type can be checked by examining the VIN code.

The Mustang GT in 2+2 fastback form (identified by the body designation carried on the front wings). GT equipment included special trim, full instumentation, driving lamps and, later, disc front brakes. This early car retains the standard Mustang fuel filler cap.

free-breathing air intake system, free-flow exhaust, solid lifters, low-restriction air cleaner and chrome-plated valve stems. Although more than ample in this 'factory' form, there were ways to coax even more power out of the brute. You could order, for example, 'Cobra equipment', including special camshafts, heads and manifolds, dual four-barrel or Weber carburettors. It was all bolt-on, 'stock' componentry, recognized by most racing organizations. Neither was it expensive. The Cobra cam kit, solid lifters and a 306-degree duration cam with .289in lift, cost only $73. The cylinder head kit (two stock 271 heads with oversize valves, heavy-duty valve springs and retainers) was $222. The engine performance kit (matched pistons combined with the previously mentioned kits) cost $343. A single four-barrel carburettor on a big-port aluminium manifold was only $120; dual fours were $240; a dual-point centrifugal distributor was a mere $50. Thus it was possible to build yourself a fairly formidable street racer for remarkably little outlay.

Bear in mind that most of the Ford horsepower figures were advertised gross, not net-on-the-dyno, and in fact a stock 271 tested by Ford produced only 232 SAE gross bhp at 5,500rpm. Lying about horsepower was one of the things the US industry used to do regularly. But a stripped-down engine with all the street accessories, fitted with special heads, centrifugal distributor, headers and three two-barrel carbs, recorded 314bhp at 6,500 on the

Rear legroom was scanty in fastbacks, but the rear seat could be folded down and the boot partition laid flat to create an enormous cargo hold. The special 'GT' fuel filler cap was introduced on 1966 models. Just visible on this car is the additional Rally-Pac comprising matching tachometer and clock just ahead of the five-dial instrumentation, which had become standard across the range that year.

dyno.

The four-speed gearbox was mandatory on the 271 engine, which was available with optional drag racing rear axle ratios of 3.89:1 and 4.11:1. Ordinarily, the ratio was 3.20:1 with the Six, 2.80:1 with the V8 two-barrels, 3.00:1 with the four-barrels and 3.50:1 with the 271 V8. It could be argued that 2.80:1 Mustangs were over-geared, but Ford was catering here to people who wanted economy and smooth highway cruising.

Front disc brakes were offered late in 1965 for only $58 extra.

Built by Kelsey-Hayes, these were one-piece cast-iron units with a disc diameter of 9½in. A radial rib separated the two braking surfaces, and each brake pad was actuated by two cylinders. Discs were valuable options because the Mustang's front drums were not noted for fade-resistance – they added an important and even vital bit of serious hardware to the V8s that they certainly should have had from the beginning.

Also in September 1964, Ford added a third body style, the 2+2, basically a semi-fastback which tapered back to a mild notch

This is a late-1965 version of the Mustang 2+2 GT featuring styled steel wheels, whitewall tyres and racing stripes between the wheel wells. The exhaust outlets have been brought well clear of the rear body panel.

partway down the boot lid. Rear leg room in the 2+2 was just what its designation suggested, but the rear seat folded down to carry luggage, creating a practical, roomy cargo compartment. The 2+2 was a token gesture towards the genuine sports car Joe Oros and others had hoped would be included in the Mustang line, though its wheelbase and overall length were no different from those of the coupe and convertible.

All Mustangs, of course, exhibited the long-bonnet/short-boot appearance which came to be known as the first criterion of ponycars. This was not, contrary to hoary myth and rumour, a particularly new distribution of body masses; the Studebaker Hawks had used similar shapes since 1956. But Ford was certainly the first company to use it successfully, and it wasn't until 1967 that arch-rivals Chevrolet and Pontiac were able to release the competitive Camaro and Firebird. Even Lincoln-Mercury had to wait until 1967 for their upmarket ponycar, the Mercury Cougar. American Motors moved rapidly, offering its Javelin by 1968, but Chrysler wasn't really in the running with a true Mustang-answer until the second-generation Barracuda in 1967.

The disadvantages of the long bonnet shape were also self-evident, though in the mid-'Sixties they were far outweighed by its

sales appeal. Long bonnets and short decks made for limited cargo space and generally poor space utilization. Eventually, this led to the decline of the ponycar in the early 'Seventies, as Americans became more interested in space-efficient designs from Europe and Japan.

Sports car people, those who had admired the Mustang I, were predictably less than enthusiastic over the production car. Standard suspension models were 'wallowy', as *Road & Track* put it: 'There's a tendency for the car to float when being driven at touring speeds, and the "porpoise" factor is high on an undulating surface... There seems little excuse for such frankly sloppy suspension on any car with the sporting characteristics which have been claimed for the Mustang...' The editors praised the car's good looks and low price and admitted that Mustangs were carpeted, trimmed and finished 'in a manner that many European sports/touring cars would do well to emulate'. But they regretted that, otherwise, it was little different from 'the typical American sedan'.

The optioned 271bhp model did better in *R&T*'s test, delivering 0-60mph from rest in 8.3 seconds, a quarter-mile time of 15.6 seconds at 85mph and a top speed of 120mph. The optional handling package (stiffer springs and shocks and a larger front anti-sway

An early Mustang convertible featuring the Falcon-derived instrument panel with horizontal speedometer markings in addition to the optional Rally-Pac dials.

bar, faster steering, 5.90 x 15 Firestone Super Sports tyres) was great, *R&T* said: 'The effect is to eliminate the wallow we experienced with previous Mustangs, and to tie the car to the road much more firmly, so on a fast run the point of one's departure into the boondocks is delayed very considerably. There is a certain harshness to the ride at low speeds over poor surfaces, but this is a small price to pay for the great improvement in handling and roadholding.' The testers noted marked oversteer on this version, even though it had 56 per cent of its weight over the front wheels. But its hard suspension 'inspired more confidence in the driver'.

The editors now cheered the H-P Mustang as 'a big step in the right direction', but still looked askance at its drum brakes and beam rear axle. Until those items were attended to, *R&T* said, it would remain 'reluctantly unconquered'. The discs showed up as an option within months, but IRS never materialized, and *R&T* was never fully conquered. Since theirs was the most negative reception the Mustang received, it is interesting to study their objections, if only to determine what the Mustang didn't provide for those Iacocca called 'the real buffs'. But not all the buffs agreed. Writing in *Popular Science*, racing driver Dan Gurney stated: 'This car will run the rubber off a Triumph or MG. It has the feel of a 2+2 Ferrari. So what *is* a sports car?' Gurney's H-P Mustang did

Although the basic design remained the same, there were subtle differences between the stock interior of the 1965 convertible immediately above and that of the GT model to the right of it, most notable being the more pronounced padding of the divider between the two rear seat cushions and backrest panels.

The standard interior of an early 1965 Mustang convertible with automatic transmission. A different shift quadrant was called for when cars were fitted with the optional centre console over the transmission tunnel.

The styled steel wheel which became a popular option in 1965, especially on GT models. Originally produced as a single pressing, it was later supplied with separate centre and outer ring, both of them chromed.

123mph and consistently beat a similarly powered Corvette in quarter-mile acceleration runs. So if Ford had not created a sports car in the truest sense, the Hi-Performance Mustang certainly came close.

The huge success of the 1965 vintage gave Ford little reason to alter the 1966 model, despite the extra-long 1965 model year. Only detail changes were made. A single horizontal grille bar was replaced by several thin bars, but the galloping horse emblem was retained in the centre of the radiator opening. The GT used a 1965-style grille with auxiliary driving lamps mounted at the ends of the horizontal bar. These were more decorative than functional, however, and are not much help to the fast driver in a GT. At the rear of the 1966 model, the fuel filler cap was redesigned, and along the sides the simulated rear wheel scoop received three wind splits. Front nameplates were integrated with emblems, and GTs had an extra badge on their front wings. Finally, the wheel covers were redesigned and a new five-slot affair adopted.

A few important changes did occur inside, where the Falcon-

A 1965 GT convertible with a four-outlet air conditioning unit mounted over the transmission tunnel. The fan and temperature controls are located between the left and right pairs of outlets, respectively.

44

based instrument panel was replaced by a needle gauge version, identical to that of the 1965 GT package. The Rally-Pac tachometer/clock combination remained optional.

Chassiswise, six-cylinder Mustangs received the 14in wheels that had been confined to V8s in 1965, and engine mounts on all models were redesigned to reduce vibration. With the 170 cid Six and 260 cid V8 eliminated, engine offerings were rationalized to four: the basic 200 cid Six and the 289 V8 in 200, 225 and 271bhp form. The option list was extended to include a stereo cartridge tape system and deluxe seat belts with a reminder lamp.

Sales for 1966 could not match 1965 because of the longer 1965 model year, but taking comparable 12-month periods, 1966 sales were actually 50,000 units higher. The Mustang was still enjoying a clear run, with Chevrolet's Camaro and Pontiac's Firebird still one year away, Corvair sales rapidly declining, and Chrysler's 'glassback' Barracudas really only lip-service competition. Thus Ford picked up close to half a million hardtop sales that year, along with 70,000 convertibles and 35,000 fastbacks. This should tell the Mustang collector something; obviously, the fastback will be – indeed is – the scarcest body style, well worth looking for. Also, in its way, the fastback is the sportiest design of the three.

Ford pushed six-cylinder Mustangs harder in 1966. For one thing, this was the price leader, with a base cost of only $2,416. Though the Six looked like its V8 brethren, it was considerably different under the skin. The wheels, though larger in 1966, had four lugs instead of the V8's five, and the standard drum brakes

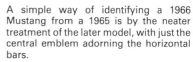

A simple way of identifying a 1966 Mustang from a 1965 is by the neater treatment of the later model, with just the central emblem adorning the horizontal bars.

The limited use of chrome enhances the side view of this 1966 convertible, although an optional 'air scoop' ornament in the body recess behind the doors was available for those who could not resist brightwork.

A styling buck of a 1966 2+2 fastback revealing the fold-flat arrangement of the rear seat for increasing luggage capacity. Note also the duotone upholstery finish, which was to figure increasingly through the Mustang range.

were 9in, not 10in units. Sixes had lighter rear axles and a slightly narrower front track than V8s. Spring rates were adjusted, too, for the Mustang Six would have looked tail-heavy if it had used the V8 suspension. The brakes were effective with this modest engine, though susceptible to fade on continuous hard applications. The Six performed well, all things considered, *Motor Trend's* automatic-equipped example handling the 0-60mph sprint in only 14.3 seconds and averaging 20 miles per US gallon on regular, low-octane petrol.

Road-testers now felt obliged to take a harder look at the two-year-old car, and writers listed a number of minor design flaws plus one serious inherent problem. The nits included lack of rear-seat ashtrays and armrests, and the omission of dashboard interior lights. The larger problem was limited passenger space in the rear – a characteristic of all ponycars. 'Five passengers can fit, but the fifth one usually sits on the other four's nerves', said *Motor Trend*, but the magazine did give the Mustang good marks as 'safe and roadworthy, easy to handle, and fun to drive'.

Together, the 1965 and 1966 Mustang comprise the first distinguishable family of cars, for changes occurred with greater rapidity in and out on the 1967s. Today, they remain the classic original, the cars most in demand by collectors, and the large supply will keep them in this desirable position for some years to come. But greater things were ahead which rendered the post-1966 models more desirable in many ways, and the potential collector should not rule them out.

CHAPTER 5

Shelby Mustangs 1965 to 1966

GT-350 and the performance image

The fleet and aggressively handsome Shelby Mustangs are beyond any doubt the most desirable and sought-after examples of the breed, especially in their first two years, when famed racing driver-turned-car builder Carroll Shelby performed his celebrated magic on the fastback version of Ford's ponycar. Alone among Mustangs at this writing, they are recognized as Milestone cars, and well they deserve to be. They proved that the attractive Mustang package was only the beginning of a formula for high performance that could be carried out to undreamed-of lengths through a little judicious tweaking by somebody who knew what he was doing.

Carroll Shelby knew, alright. Father of the Cobra, he had begun racing sports cars in the 'Fifties, progressing from MGs to Ferraris, Maseratis and Aston Martins. He was a good driver, but not wealthy, and prize money was nothing to speak of in those days. Purely on the strength of his driving, though, Shelby attracted the necessary sponsors, and by the time he won the 24 Hours of Le Mans for Aston Martin in 1959 he was one of the most celebrated and in-demand drivers in the world. Alas, heart trouble forced him into retirement soon after this peak performance. Since he could no longer race, Shelby decided to build cars; maybe we have something to thank his old ticker for, after all.

Shelby settled in southern California and made cars his business. First, he bought a Goodyear tyre distributorship. Then, he started the first high-performance driving school in the US. He also nurtured a private dream: He would build a car of his own, someday – the world's fastest production sports car. But without capital, and no firm design ideas, Shelby's vision remained only that. Later, fate took a hand. Shelby had heard that Ford was developing a small lightweight V8 engine, the famous Fairlane 221

– later enlarged to 260 and eventually to 289 cubic inches. At about the same time, it was learned that AC Cars, of Surrey, England, was about to go out of business since the firm had lost its engine supplier for its strong, lightweight Ace sports car. Shelby stepped in at precisely the right moment, dropped the Ford engine into the AC sports car, and the Cobra was born.

Cobra soon became a household word – at least in the households of car enthusiasts. In their minds, the Shelby name became inextricably linked to Ford's performance image in the early and middle 'Sixties, and Cobra became synonymous with horsepower. The reason: Cobras were winning almost every race in sight, including the coveted World Manufacturer's Championship for GT cars, a title which was held by Ferrari for 12 years before it was grudgingly yielded to Shelby.

The Cobra rub-off on to Ford's regular product line was of enormous value to Dearborn. Ford had already discovered the youth market and had launched the Mustang to capture it. Though initial Mustang sales had been higher than anyone at Ford had expected, the car lacked a distinct high-performance image. Thus Ford asked Shelby to race Mustangs against the Corvettes in Sports Car Club of America (SCCA) competition – and to please win. Flushed with the Cobra's success, and knowing his way around race tracks and sanctioning bodies, Shelby had a predictable reply: 'Build a hundred of 'em.' That was the minimum number which had to be built in order for a car to qualify (or be homologated) as a Production-class racer.

As a first step, Shelby built two prototypes that started out as ordinary Mustang fastbacks. A team of engineers and development drivers made numerous changes which transformed the soft,

Carroll Shelby based his Shelby Mustangs on the 2+2 fastback body. The car on the left is a 1966 model, with additional rear quarter windows in plastic to improve vision and extra air scoops behind the doors to assist rear brake cooling. The 1967 car on the right features a substantially restyled fastback profile and optional 10-spoke alloy wheels. Both are GT-350s.

A Shelby Mustang GT-350 in its natural environment, being accelerated hard out of a tight turn and revealing minimal body lean.

The plain grille with offset Mustang motif is a familiar Shelby feature, as are the twin racing strips running the length of the car, one each side of the centreline, and matched by narrow styling strips along the bottom of the doors and body sides.

boulevard sporty cars into muscular racers that still looked a lot like the production Mustang. After all, if Ford was going to get any publicity benefit from its racing effort, the cars would still need to be recognizable as Mustangs. Another goal of the Shelby programme was to develop a Ford alternative to the Corvette. (The Cobra, although sold through selected Ford dealers, had always been regarded as an AC or a Shelby, not a Ford.)

Once the final specification for Shelby's redesigned Mustang had been determined, a dozen white fastbacks were built at the Cobra production facility in Venice, California, in late 1964. Another 100 white fastbacks ready for conversion were soon shipped to Venice from Ford's San Jose, California assembly plant. When SCCA inspectors arrived at the Shelby workshops to approve the model for production racing, they were somewhat surprised to find that more than the required minimum of 100 cars had been completed.

Just what did Shelby do to create these very special Mustangs? The formula was never a secret. These cars were certainly different from their mass-production brothers, but they still looked like Mustangs, and that was important. It was this similiarity in appearance that allowed the excitement of the Shelby Mustangs to rub off on to the more ordinary models. As a result, Ford's ponycar got exactly the kind of performance image the company wanted.

The Shelby formula was to start with a Mustang specially built to be modified by the Shelby factory and supplied with as many Ford parts as possible (although not necessarily Mustang parts). Each car to be converted was delivered by Ford as a white fastback with a black interior, 271bhp Hi-Performance engine, four-speed all-synchromesh transmission, Ford Galaxie rear end, and a long list of 'delete items'. Shelby-bound Mustangs were produced without bonnet, exhaust system, or rear seats. On the Shelby

The major changes in the profile of the 1967 Shelby GT-350 compared with the 1966 model are clearly defined in these two illustrations. The additional driving lamps on the later car were installed by its owner, Jim Inglese.

assembly line, each car received extensive suspension modifications, Koni shock absorbers, aluminium high-rise intake manifolds, finned aluminium valve covers and oil pan, special Holley carburettor, large front anti-sway bar, and a glassfibre hood with a functioning air scoop. Interior appointments included 3in competition seat belts, a tachometer and oil pressure gauge mounted at eye level on the dashboard, and a wood-rimmed flat-dish racing-type steering wheel. Since there was no rear seat, the spare tyre was relocated to the empty space for better weight distribution.

All 1965 Shelbys were white with black interior – no other colours were used. They could also be identified (all Ford and Mustang emblems were removed), by their blue rocker panel racing stripes which displayed the car's name – GT-350. Most of the early Shelby Mustangs also had optional 10in wide 'Le Mans' stripes, which ran from front to rear over the top of the car and were also blue. (American international racing colours are blue and white.)

Shelby's Mustang was originally conceived as a racing car, but most of those built saw duty on the street. Because Shelby realized that he could not easily sell 100 *bona fide* racing cars, he offered a standard model nearly identical in appearance with the racing version.

The most important feature of the R-model racer was the engine. SCCA rules specified that to qualify for Production racing, a car's suspension or engine could be modified, but not both. Shelby chose to keep the same suspension components for both the street and the competition versions of the GT-350 so that, under the rules, he could modify the engine. The street engine was based on Ford's 271bhp Hi-Performance 289, but used a hot cam, a large carburettor and a less restrictive exhaust. It yielded an honest 306bhp. But the racing car engine also had special heads, and was rated at between 340 and 360bhp. The racing cars also weighed only 2,500lb, compared to 2,800lb for the street machines.

The GT-350 was homologated for SCCA B-Production, which meant it would compete against small-block Corvettes, Sunbeam Tigers, Jaguar E-types and the occasional Ferrari or Aston Martin. In total 562 Shelby Mustangs were built as 1965 models, but no more than 30 of these were built to racing specification. However, since all the special parts were available to private customers over the counter (per Shelby philosophy), anyone could turn their street car into the racing model by removing and/or substituting parts. Many owners did just that.

On Shelby Mustangs the normal Ford VIN number stamped on the left frame rail is obscured by a plate carrying the familiar Carroll Shelby motif, the vehicle serial number and confirmation that the car was a product of Shelby American Inc., of Los Angeles, California. The plate is located just forward of the engine compartment's transverse tie-bar.

The GT-350 quickly established itself as the car to beat in B-Production and it captured the national class championship from 1965 through to 1967. Because GT-350s were so successful, it was naturally assumed that a lot of them were competing. In fact, there weren't. What spectators saw were the same cars winning time after time. And, since the street cars looked so much like the racers, everyone assumed that they were all alike under the skin. This, of course, was a real ego boost for owners of the street cars, not to mention Ford Division.

To sell his earlier Cobra sports car, Shelby had established a network of performance-oriented Ford dealers, and he used this tactic again to get GT-350s into customer hands quickly. Although touted as 'not the car for everybody', they sold as rapidly as they could be built. The demand quickly exceeded the production capacity of Shelby's plant, which was also still making the Cobra.

The normal five-dial instrumentation on 1966 Shelby Mustangs was augmented by an oil pressure gauge and tachometer in an additional housing over the centre of the dashboard, just above the radio.

By the spring of 1965, the newly named Shelby American Incorporated had moved from its Venice facility to two huge hangars on the edge of the Los Angeles International Airport.

The first batch of GT-350 street machines were made available to members of the automotive press for road-testing. Virtually every major publication reported on the car, but because it had no obvious competitor, most journalists could do little more than describe the GT-350 and its sizzling performance. GT-350s were loud, rough-riding, and a real effort to drive. But the driver was rewarded by the car's instant response. Function was the key word. Anything that did not contribute to the car's purpose – to go fast, handle well and stop quickly – was either modified or thrown out.

In 1965, the Shelby GT-350 sold for $4,547, which was about $1,000 more than an optional Mustang GT and an equal amount less than the Corvette. This pricing put it right in the middle of the performance market. With 0-60mph averaging 6.5 seconds, a top speed of 130 to 135mph and race car handling and braking, the car drew rave reviews. It soon became something of a legend, and began to influence Detroit. Suddenly, scoops and rocker panel stripes began appearing on all sorts of production cars. While other manufacturers never actually offered a car in the same league as the GT-350, quite a few thought they did.

At the time the 1966 Shelby Mustang was being planned, a lot was also happening at Ford. The company's all-out exotic performance car, the Ford GT, was faltering in international competition, so responsibility for the GT racing programme was handed over to Carroll Shelby. Ford wanted the GT to carry its banner to the winner's circle at race tracks around the world. Since the company had invested a lot of money and faith in Shelby American, it

A pronounced lip to the housing of the additional instruments on Shelby models does much to minimize reflections.

wanted to see a tangible return on its investment – a competitive Ford GT. Shelby had a lot more on his mind in 1966 than the GT-350 alone.

Feedback from dealers and customers influenced some of the design changes made to the 1966 GT-350. The '65 was a good car, but without a back seat it was too impractical for the buyer with a family. (The rear seat had been omitted not merely so that the spare tyre could be relocated, but also to qualify the GT-350 under SCCA rules.) Also, the noisy, lurching Detroit 'Locker' rear end was unnerving to those not acquainted with it. It howled and clunked at low speeds. The side-exit exhaust system was *very* loud – and illegal in some states – and the policy of 'any colour you want, so long as it's white' did not appeal to some buyers. From Ford came a demand for something called cost-effectiveness: Can the cost of each item or modification be justified by sales? Meantime, the Shelby people were trying to explain roadability to the accountants.

In effect, the changes made to the 1966 GT-350 were brought about by buyers and potential buyers – not by Carroll Shelby. In

Special valve covers with the words 'COBRA POWERED BY FORD' cast into them immediately identify this as a Shelby Mustang. The sticker on the chromed top of the air cleaner attached to the Holley carburettor confirms that a 289 cid V8 is nestling beneath which, in standard GT-350 tune, was rated at 306 bhp.

concept and as a finished car, the 1966 model was not the sort of thing Ol' Shel would have built if the choice had been left up to him alone. Shelby buyers seemed to want performance all right, but without sacrificing other automotive virtues. So, starting in 1966, the Shelby Mustang began to evolve into a car with broader market appeal. And as more cars were sold each year, the Shelby became more like the standard Mustangs and less like the semi-race car it started out to be.

Most of the revisions of the 1966 model could have been carried out on Ford's assembly line. However, Shelby did not always incorporate specific changes with the first car of a new model year. Instead, parts on hand were used up before new parts were ordered. Thus, there is no clear distinction between 1965 and 1966 models – appropriate for a limited-production manufacturer like Shelby. The first 250 1966 models (approximately) were left-over 1965s. They received all the 1966 cosmetic touches – a new grille, side scoops and rear quarter windows – but they retained the 1965 suspension, Koni shocks and 1965-style interior, and all were still painted white.

When actual 1966 production began, colour choices were expanded to red, blue, green and black, all offered with white racing stripes. A fold-down rear seat, standard on Mustang fastbacks, became a Shelby option. Almost all the 1966 GT-350s had it for an obvious reason; it was easier, and more profitable, for Ford to leave it in during initial assembly than for Shelby to remove the seat and install a one-piece glass-fibre rear shelf. Batteries were left in their stock under-bonnet location. Heavy-duty Ford-installed shock absorbers were still used, as were the special Pitman idler arms that gave the 1965 its sharp steering. The 1965 and early 1966 Shelbys used rear traction bars, which ran from the inside of the car to the top of the rear axle; later models used Traction Master under-ride bars. Early cars also had lowered front A-arms, which altered the steering geometry for improved cornering. This refine-ment was determined not to be 'cost effective', so it was discon-tinued on later '66 cars.

Engines and drivelines remained the same. The Detroit Locker rear end was made optional, as was an automatic transmission. All '66s, like '65s, used large disc brakes at the front and large drums with sintered metallic linings at the rear. Extra pedal pressure was required with these brakes, but they just didn't fade. The early 15in mag wheels (actually aluminium centres with steel rims) were replaced by 14in rims. These were either chrome-styled steel or cast-aluminium alloy wheels, at the buyer's option. All '66s received Plexiglas rear quarter windows in place of the Mustang fastback's stock louvres used on '65 Shelbys.

Increased production was planned for 1966, so that every Shelby dealer who wanted cars could get them. Shelby also sold the Hertz Company on the idea of buying about 1,000 special GT-350H cars, all of which were finished in black with gold stripes. Hertz rented them at major airports throughout 1966. A lot of them were returned from a weekend's rental with definite signs of having been used in competition. Not surprisingly, Hertz soon found the GT-350H programme a mite unprofitable.

Shelby Mustang production in the second year was 2,380, including 936 Hertz models and six specially-built convertibles, which Shelby gave away as gifts at the end of the model year. No racing cars were constructed, though a few left-over '65s were registered as 1966s. Shelbys continued to race and win that year, although they were essentially the same cars that had run the year before.

While the 1966 GT-350 wasn't quite as loud or fierce as the previous version, Shelby nevertheless kept it interesting. As an option, he offered a Paxton centrifugal supercharger. (A special GT-350S was envisaged, but never actually released.) The Paxton-blown engine was advertised with a horsepower increase of 'up to 46 per cent'.

CHAPTER 6

Mustangs 1967 to 1968

Longer, wider and smoother

You think *you* have troubles! In 1967 Ford Division had the Camaro, Firebird and new Barracuda to contend with. They also had a three-year-old phenomenon that was suddenly old hat, faced with an all-new engineering, styling and publicity onslaught by the biggest corporation in the world, which had taken only slightly more than two years to field two Mustang-substitutes. And the Camaro and Firebird were good cars – darn good.

While there may have been substitutes for Mustangs that year, there was no substitute, as the stock car driver said, for cubic inches. 'Cubes' were the formula by which Ford hoped to remain top of the ponycar heap. The formula was a new, much larger four-barrel V8, 390 cubic inches (4.05 x 3.78in), developing 320 horsepower, borrowed intact from the Thunderbird and now optional on the Mustang. Ford recommended that 390s be teamed with Select-Shift Cruise-O-Matic, a gear-hold three-speed automatic capable of handling the power of this big mill. In all, there were now 13 different Mustang power teams, beginning with the 200 cid Six and three-speed manual gearbox and working up through the 289s to the big-block 390.

Unfortunately, the 390 V8 was also a heavy engine; it gave the Mustang a 58/42 weight distribution and the cars understeered with merry abandon. Ford fitted Firestone F70-14 Wide-Oval tyres as standard, but it didn't help all that much and the 289s were far nimbler cars. Ford did not standardize the competition handling package, but if you ordered a 390 you did well to go for it. The kit included stiffer springs, a thicker front sway bar, Koni shocks, limited-slip differential, quick steering and 15in wheels. Also available for the 271bhp 289, this package improved handling, but gave the car a stiff buckboard ride that was less than ideal on

America's beat-up secondary roads.

The 289 was by far a better all-round Mustang, but there was no gainsaying the 390's performance. Zero to 60mph came in 7.5 seconds flat, the standing quarter-mile in 15.5 at 95mph, and top speed was about 120mph. It was a car built for the heavy-of-foot, more at home on the dragstrip than on winding backwoods roads, where indeed it was quite a handful.

Ford didn't pursue an entirely new body style for 1967, but Design Staff managed to alter the cars from the beltline down. Fastbacks received a sweeping new roof line, now a full fastback blending cleanly into the rear deck and ending in a Kamm-back tail. A few extra inches were added to the front overhang, and the bizarre 'gills' on either side of the grille opening on 1965-66 cars were eliminated. The new car was also wider, by 2½in, and had a 2in wider track than its predecessors. Further reduction of noise and vibration was managed by adding new rubber bushings to suspension attachment points.

The key alteration was the wider track – done mainly to provide room for 390 installation, it improved the handling of all models. At the same time, the front springs were relocated above the top crossmember, per Fairlane practice, and the upper A-arm pivots were lowered. The roll centre was raised – this tactic was gleaned from Shelby, who had used it to good effect on his GT-350s. On 289 Mustangs, understeer was reduced since the outside front wheel was held exactly perpendicular to the road when cornering. Since the change did not mandate stiffer front spring rates, the ride of the standard-suspension cars did not suffer.

Against its small army of competitors the 1967 Mustang compared favourably. Its economical six-cylinder engine was easier on

The 1967 Mustangs marked the first significant change in appearance since the introduction of the series more than two years earlier. At the front, horizontal and vertical bars protruded from the central motif of a much deeper grille, which now had a rectangular mesh pattern, while at the rear, the luggage compartment lid was stepped to accentuate taller and concave-shaped triple rear lights.

The major restyle introduced for 1967 was accompanied by a 390 cid engine option. The hardtop shown here, as well as the convertible, were changed from the beltline down, receiving deeper side sculpture as well as a longer nose. They were 2.5in wider than previous models, but retained the same wheelbase.

Almost there. This styling proposal for the interior of the 1967 Mustang came very close to the production specification. A tilt-away steering wheel, adjustable in the vertical plane and able to be moved sideways with the ignition switched off, was to join the long list of options.

petrol than the Barracuda's or Camaro's, and still provided surprisingly good performance. Model for model, the Mustang was usually lighter than the Camaro/Firebird and Barracuda, and yielded both better economy and higher performance with comparable drivetrains. And Ford was offering a wider selection of V8s than its competitors, although Camaro's optional 396 V8 with 375bhp had the edge even on the 390 Mustang.

But the competition had gained in the design area by dint of two extra years' development time; the Barracuda had more room and better access through its opening fastback hatch. Despite continual efforts at noise reduction, the Mustang was noisier and somewhat harsher riding than the GM or Chrysler ponycars. The Mustang scored in details, with its swing-away steering wheel option and genuine glass convertible backlight, which was better by far than plastic.

One area Mustang couldn't overcome was styling. The Camaro, Firebird and Barracuda were by definition *new* cars, while the Mustang, though somewhat altered, still bore a close resemblance to its mid-1964 predecessor. Finally, it had another rival from within its own corporate hierarchy, the Mercury Cougar, although the Cougar was carefully designed to a price rather higher than

Twin foglamps mounted within the grille continued to be a feature of GT-specification Mustangs following the body changes introduced for 1967.

The 1967 fastback received a sweeping new roofline, which blended cleanly into the rear deck, thereby losing the notched appearance of the previous 2+2.

The extensively revised interior of a 1967 convertible. Matching large speedometer and tachometer dials dominated the revised instrument layout of most cars, but when the optional tachometer was omitted a combined oil pressure gauge and alternator took its place.

A further grille revision was introduced for 1968 with an inner ring following the contours of the outer frame.

Neat rocker panel mouldings were standard equipment on convertibles and fastbacks in 1968, but these 16-spoke wheel trims were one of several designs on the options list. A major mechanical change that year was the substitution of the Hi-Performance 289 cid engine by the longer-stroke 302 cid V8.

Mustang's by upmarket-oriented Lincoln-Mercury. The inevitable result was lower Mustang sales, down approximately 25 per cent from 1966, mostly in the hardtop area. The snappy new fastback was twice as popular as before, selling 70,000 units, while the Mustang convertible, like all American convertibles by that time, was heading toward eclipse with 45,000 sales. Despite the competition, though, 472,121 sales of 1967 models was hardly anything to sniff at, particularly for a three-year-old design. But it wouldn't last.

In 1968, Mustang sales plummeted despite a year of improved volume for the US industry and Ford Division as a whole, and despite the largest assortment of engines and other options in Mustang history. This has conversely made the 1968 Mustang an interesting car for the collector; if you somehow couldn't manage to 'option' one exactly the way you wished in the past three years, you certainly could do so in 1968.

The factors behind the decline by over 150,000 sales in 1968 had to do with the competition more than the net worth of Ford's ponycar. Now American Motors had joined the fray with its fine new Javelin and short-wheelbase AMX. GM and Chrysler had

The Mustang hardtop for 1968 with full wheel covers. A simplified form of decorative trim was adopted for the body sides of standard-specification cars. A 427 cid V8 engine option was offered for a brief period.

Distinctive wheel covers help to identify this 1968 fastback GT and a new accent stripe emphasizes the simulated air scoop between door and rear wheel.

Contrasting-coloured exit panels from the optional bonnet louvres of this 1968 convertible suggest a high-performance image, but the lack of foglamps in the grille means that this car is not, in fact, a GT.

For 1968, too, Mustang styling wasn't much changed. The three body styles were continued, with new rear quarter-panels carrying fake air scoops ahead of the rear wheels. Crease lines ran back from the upper front wing around the rear scoop and back forward again into the lower part of the doors. On GT models the sculpture was accented with tape striping – for better or worse. The grille was revised, deeply inset, with a bright ring around the now-familiar galloping pony. GT foglamps were again carried inside the grille opening. GT equipment was essentially unchanged from 1967, but now included the side striping, dual exhausts with chrome-plated quad outlets, a pop-open petrol cap, H-D suspension, F70-14 whitewall tyres on 6in rims and styled steel wheels. Wide-Oval tyres could also be ordered.

Some of the 1968 engines had to be altered to meet the new Federal emissions standards which went into effect that year. The compression ratio of the Six was lowered from 9.2:1 to 8.8:1 and horsepower dropped to 115. The two-barrel 289 V8 was also reduced in compression and rated at 195, not 200bhp. The 390 V8, however, went to 335bhp. The higher-performance 289 now gave way to a 302 V8, which produced 230bhp and cost an extra $200. For an extra $755 you could now order the huge 427 V8 from the standard-sized cars, which had a 10.9:1 compression and developed 390 gross horsepower. Standard transmission was the three-speed manual all-synchro gearbox, and the 271 V8 continued with a choice of four-speed or Cruise-O-Matic. The 427 could be ordered only with Cruise-O-Matic.

Ford made much of safety features that year, though most of them were mandatory: energy-absorbing instrument panel and steering column, retractable seat belts front and rear, reversing lamps, dual-circuit brake system, hazard warning flashers, side marker lights, energy-absorbing seat backs, self-locking folding seats, positive door lock buttons, safety door handles, double-yoke door latches, padded sun visors and windshield pillars, double-thick laminated windscreen, day/night rear-view mirror on a breakaway mounting, outside rear-view mirror, safety-rim wheels and load-rated tyres were all standard. So were corrosion-resistant brake lines and a standardized shift quadrant for the automatic transmission. To meet glare reduction standards, the windscreen wiper arms, steering wheel hub and horn ring, rear-view mirror mounting and windshield pillars were dull-finished. Carried over from 1967 were reversible keys and a 6,000-mile lube and oil-

upped the ante with new variations of their own sporty cars, and here was also the problem of price. The 1968 Mustang convertible was listed at over $2,800, and a handful of performance options could raise the fob to over $4,000, which was a long way from $2,365. Even the sporty fastback model suffered – in part from Ford's own intermediate Torino fastback, the replacement for the 1967 Fairlane 500XL and GT musclecars. The Torino was visibly larger than the Mustang and its 116in wheelbase afforded a roomy back seat. The Torino accounted for nearly 54,000 sales in 1968, and some of these were certainly taken from Mustang fastbacks.

A well-equipped 1968 Mustang GT 2+2 fastback. 'GT' identification was provided on the body sides, in the centre of the wheel trims and on the fuel filler cap. Heavy-duty suspension, including stiffer springs and a larger front anti-sway bar, was also part of the GT package, together with dual outlets for each exhaust pipe.

Head restraints have been added to this 1968 convertible, the cover for the folded top of which offers a particularly tidy appearance. Note the slightly concave profile of the rear body panel.

change interval.

Like all Fords that year, the Mustang came with a 5/50-24/24 warranty: powertrain, suspension, steering and wheels were warranted for five years or 50,000 miles, whichever came first; other components were guaranteed for 24 months or 24,000 miles. The second purchaser could transfer the unused portion of the warranty for a fee not exceeding $25.

At its price the 427 Mustang was a rare beast, and it carried an engine that was arguably too much for the car. While 427s could leap from rest to 60mph in just 6 or 7 seconds, they were ponderous oversteerers, more so even than the 390s. The latter had the benefit of being available with manual transmission, so it was – and is – a better all-round choice for the Mustang driver interested in straight-line performance.

The 390 Mustangs also benefited in 1968 from floating-caliper power front disc brakes, which were an extra-cost item, but mandatory. These provided more stopping force with no increase in pedal pressure from the 1967 variety. The floating caliper design promoted longer brake life because it used fewer parts than previous discs; they were also a required option on 427 Mustangs.

At over 300,000 units for 1968, Mustang sales were well down for the first time, but Ford Division wasn't unduly worried. Since 1966, plans had been made for new products, and all these came together in model year 1969. The basic body package and 108in wheelbase were retained, but the Mustang line was completely overhauled so as to compete more evenly in the new luxury and performance areas of the ponycar market. The 1969 Mustang Grande was the luxury entry, and in the performance field enthusiasts would welcome a Mustang that made fresh history – the fiery Mach I.

CHAPTER 7

Shelby Mustangs 1967 to 1970

GT-350, GT-500 and GT-500KR

For 1967, production Mustangs were larger, heavier and more 'styled'. This meant the GT-350 would also have to change. To keep the car's weight down and its appearance distinctive, Shelby stylists created a glassfibre front end to complement the production Mustang's longer bonnet. They also put two high-beam headlamps in the centre of the grille opening. (Some later cars have these lamps moved to the outer ends of the grille to comply with state motor vehicle requirements specifying a minimum distance between headlamps.) The 1967 Shelbys had a larger hood scoop and sculptured brake cooling scoops on the sides. Another set of scoops on the rear-quarter roof panels acted as interior air extractors. The rear end received a spoiler and a large bank of taillamps. As a total design the 1967 Shelby was stunning. It looked more like a racing car than many racers; there was still nothing like it.

Because the '67 was heavier than its predecessors, and because customer feedback indicated a preference for a more manageable car, power steering and power brakes were mandatory options. The new interior received some special appointments not shared with the production Mustang including a distinctive racing steering wheel, additional gauges and a genuine rollbar with inertia-reel shoulder harnesses.

In 1967, Ford offered a 390 cid V8 for its standard Mustang as its top performance engine. In typical Shelby style, Carroll went one better with a 428 cubic-incher and a new model, the GT-500. It was a highly popular move, for GT-500s outsold GT-350s by a two-to-one margin. The GT-350 still carried the 271bhp engine warmed to Shelby specifications, but now without the steel-tube exhaust headers.

What Shelby had now created was a combination of perfor-mance and luxury, cars that no longer emphasized performance above everything else. Since car makers adopted more conservative horsepower ratings in 1967 – mainly to keep the insurance companies happy – the GT-500 was rated at only 355bhp, although it certainly developed more than that. The GT-350 was still rated at 306bhp, which is odd because without the headers and straight-through mufflers the output was certainly lower than this. No attempt was made by the factory to race the 1967 models. Altogether, 3,225 of them were built and sold.

By 1968, Carroll Shelby was beginning to tire of the car business. He'd won the Manufacturers Championship and had over-seen the Ford GT effort, culminating with wins at Le Mans in 1966 and 1967. He had also seen many close friends lose their lives on the race track. Meanwhile, competition had grown and new racing technology made it impossible for all but a few specialists to grasp new principles and apply them successfully. Racing, Shelby decided, wasn't fun anymore. It was business, and building his own cars had lost much of its original attraction because Ford was now calling most of the shots.

At the end of the 1967 model run. Shelby production was moved from Los Angeles to Michigan. The A.O. Smith Company was contracted to carry out Shelby conversions on stock Mustangs and Ford handled all promotion and advertising. The '68 Shelby received a facelift: a new bonnet and nose, sequential rear turn signals and a built-in rollbar for the convertible. GT-350s used Ford's new 302 cid engine. Luxury options like automatic transmission, air conditioning, tilt-type steering wheel, tinted glass and AM-FM stereo now outnumbered performance features. In mid-year, the 428 cid engine was replaced with the 428 Cobra Jet unit, which had

The 1968 model year brought a change of production venue from California to Michigan for Shelby Mustangs as well as further changes of style. The new glassfibre bonnet provided dual inlets closer to the nose of the car with extractor vents behind them.

For 1968 only both the GT-350 and GT-500 were marketed as Shelby Cobras and carried snake badges on the front wings. The revised rear lights treatment had been borrowed from an earlier Thunderbird design.

made a name for itself on drag strips. Cars with this engine were called GT-500KR ('King of the Road') and replaced the GT-500. Again in 1968, the big-block Shelbys were more popular, outselling the GT-350s by two-to-one. Total 1968 production was 4,450 cars.

By 1969, the Federal Government had introduced the first engine emission and safety regulations. Meanwhile, insurance premiums in the region of $1,000 were being quoted for 25-year-old males who drove quick cars. The taste of buyers had changed, too – performance was becoming less important than luxury.

An additional Shelby model for 1968 was the GT-500KR, standing for King of the Road and featuring the 428 cid Cobra Jet engine. Appropriate badging was carried on the front wings above the model designation integrated with the body side stripes.

Like other models in the 1968 Shelby range, this GT-500KR had sequential rear turn indicators. Production of KR models that year amounted to 1,246 cars.

A convertible had been added to the Shelby series in 1968 and for 1969 it appeared with a new grille and glassfibre bonnet and front wings. Rear air scoops were mounted at wheel height on this body.

The 1969 GT-500 with recently renamed SportsRoof bodywork. Note the higher-mounted rear air scoops. The front bodywork changes increased the length by more than 3in.

Shelby saw the handwriting on the wall. Ever the individualist, he had begun by building the car he himself wanted to drive. He didn't like decisions made by committees where accountants and lawyers usually overruled the engineers and test drivers. And the niche he had created for his cars in the Ford line-up was gradually being filled by production Mustangs like the luxury Grande and the high-performance Mach I and Boss 302.

Mustang changed in 1969, and once more the Shelby changed with it. Shelby's stylists made the heavier, longer, busier production car look considerbly more rakish. They extended the bonnet, fitted a glassfibre front end with a large grille cavity, used glassfibre front fenders for reduced weight, clipped off the tail and added a spoiler and sequential turn signals. The GT-350 received the new 351 Windsor (Ontario) engine, while the 428 CJ engine continued for the GT-500. The KR designation was dropped but convertibles were still available. As usual, GT-500s outsold GT-350s and the total number of 1969 cars built was 3,150. Fuel injection had been considered for these cars, but was never adopted. A moonroof and reclining seats were other ideas that never made it into production.

At the end of the '69 model year, Carroll Shelby called it quits. Production and design had become more Ford's responsibility than his and competition from other cars built by Ford Division and other auto makers was much keener. His cars weren't being raced much anymore and the later models were no longer the kind of cars he'd envisaged in the beginning. Ford Division Executive Vice President Lee Iacocca agreed to terminate the Shelby programme. Cars still in the production pipeline at the end of 1969 were given Boss 302 front spoilers, black hood panels and new 1970 serial numbers. A little over 600 were made. Just like that, it was over.

After 1970, each succeeding year seemed to bring a less inspiring crop of cars as performance was redefined by Detroit. But as compression ratios were lowered and 0-60mph times increased, many began to see the cars of Carroll Shelby in a new light. They became collector's items and their value started to increase. Today, a Shelby is worth over twice what it sold for new. And there's justice in that.

CHAPTER 8

Mustangs 1969 to 1970

Another restyle and a SportsRoof

Collectibility of the somewhat revised but still in character 'third phase' Mustangs is sure to increase. It is simply a matter of time. The time will come – though it seems far off today – when the supply of pre-1969 models will run out, and values will start to escalate beyond even some of the current outlandish asking prices ($20,000-plus, says one report). Of course, there are several special Mustangs from the 1969-70 period which are collectible now. As for the more mundane variations, you may find a sleeper or two among them, a car that will provide reliable, sporty transport while you're waiting for it to come into its own on the collector market.

Ford had little to be ashamed about in this two-year run of ponycars, for they were largely influenced by Semon E. 'Bunkie' Knudsen, who became Ford President in early 1968 and vigorously pushed the company-backed competition projects while instilling high style and higher performance in the production models. Thus we have Knudsen, and Knudsen people, to thank for the model diversification which brought us the luxurious Grande and the high-performance Mach I and Boss 302.

The 1969 cars retained the original wheelbase, but dimensions were generally changed throughout. So was their overall roadability; car for car, a '69 handled better than its comparable predecessor, and the Cobra Jet Mach I and Boss 302 were the fastest non-Shelby Mustangs yet produced.

In leaving General Motors to join Ford, Bunkie Knudsen accomplished an historic turnabout; his father, William S. 'Big Bill' Knudsen, had left Ford after an argument with old Henry and gone to Chevrolet in the 'Twenties, soon building that GM Division into a force which rivalled and then eclipsed Ford itself. Nearly half a century later, his son thought it was a reasonable idea

to achieve the opposite, and he made a fine try. Yet Knudsen didn't clean house at Ford the way he had been expected to; he worked with the good talent at hand, while floating new design, engineering and sales projects where he saw they were needed.

In the Mustang's case, Knudsen knew he had to give the now-ageing design a fast shot in the arm, particularly in view of those formidable GM rivals, the Camaro Z/28 and Pontiac Firebird TransAm. He told the stylists to come up with lower, sleeker, fastbacked cars, while not deserting the long-bonnet/short-boot concept that the Mustang had made such a success. He denied any intention to build a true sports car (much relieving Chevrolet Division), but he left all his other options wide open, including the possibility of a mid-engined 2+2. Knudsen did admit that the market was a lot more crowded, which was only realistic. To those who pointed to the car's steady decline in sales since 1965, he said: 'We are comparing today's Mustang penetration with the penetration of the Mustang when there was no-one else in that particular segment of the market.'

Styling *did* experience a shake-up when Bunkie hired Larry Shinoda away from GM and placed him in charge of Ford's Special Design Center, assisted by a crack team including Harvey Winn, Ken Dowd, Bill Shannon and Dick Petit. Together with engineers like Chuck Mountain and Ed Hall, Shinoda concocted eye-openers like the King Cobra (a rapid Torino fastback). He also applied his background knowledge and experience with aerodynamics to the Mustang, proposing spoilers, smooth noses, airfoils and air dams, many of which actually appeared in production.

Given the normal three-year lead time for new designs, Shinoda wasn't able to affect the lines of the 1969 model very much, but this

The 1969 Mustang Grande was a move into a more luxurious field, but sales were not impressive at 22,182, which makes the Grande a car worth finding today. It came only as a notchback hardtop.

Improvements in the 1969 convertible top folding mechanism made possible a nearly flush appearance when the top was folded down.

The 1969 Mustang dashboard received the dual-cockpit treatment with instruments deeply recessed. When the optional tachometer was ordered it occupied the matching large recess to the right of the speedometer.

The Mach I was the new performance-oriented Mustang for 1969. Available with a 335bhp 428 cid Cobra Jet Ram Air engine, the Mach I featured GT handling suspension, colour-keyed dual racing mirrors and special ornamentation and striping.

Racing-type exposed bonnet locking pins were part of the Mach I's standard equipment and high-back bucket seats were part of the interior package. The major body restyling had increased the Mustang's overall length by more than 4in.

car had already been thoroughly gone over. It was 4in longer, mainly through front overhang, and was also slightly wider and lower. The grille was similar to that of previous cars, but now featured quad headlamps in place of the optional and mainly ineffective foglamps. The body side sculpture had disappeared and the vertical taillamp clusters were laid on a flat tail instead of a concave panel. The fuel tank capacity was increased from 17 to 20 (US) gallons. On the inside, the '69 was an important 2½in wider at the shoulder measurement and had 1½in more hip room, thanks to thinner doors. A modified frame crossmember under the front seat allowed rear seat leg-room to be increased by 2½in, and the boot capacity was larger, though still not very generous. The basic line-up of hardtop, fastback and convertible was retained, but many new variations were to appear, and two of them were in the showrooms at the beginning of the model year, in September 1968.

The first of these was the six- and eight-cylinder Mustang Grande hardtop, priced about $230 above the standard hardtop

and aimed at the luxury models of Firebird and intramural rival Cougar. (Knudsen considered Lincoln-Mercury almost as serious a rival as the GM makes.) The Grande came as standard with vinyl-covered roof, special identifying script, twin colour-keyed outside rear-view mirrors, wire wheel covers, bright metal trim around wheel wells, bright rocker panels and rear deck mouldings, and a two-tone paint stripe below the beltline. Its interior was decorated with a very good copy of teak wood, and the body used about 55lb of extra sound-deadening insulation.

'Companion special' to the Grande was the V8 Mach I, starting at $3,139 and aimed at the boy-racer crowd. It featured as standard simulated rear-quarter air scoops, a rear spoiler and a functional bonnet scoop (nicknamed 'The Shaker' by Ford engineers because it vibrated madly at high rpm, being attached directly to the engine air cleaner).

Dimensionally, the Mach I was little different from other '69s, but its trim and detailing made it the raciest looking Mustang in

The basic six-cylinder hardtop with hubcaps, whitewall tyres and few other options cost only $2,635, but sales of V8s far exceeded those of Sixes.

The revised body styling brought a return to a much cleaner and neater tail treatment, somewhat reminiscent of the earliest Mustangs.

A 1969 hardtop featuring deluxe seating and door trim. The upper portion of the seat backs consisted of six vinyl-covered pads. This car also has the deluxe three-spoke steering wheel.

A 1969 SportsRoof with the GT Equipment Group—the last year that this was to be offered as an optional package. Body side stripes without any lettering and 'GT' wheel centres are identification features.

Another angle on the 1969 GT. Twin leads extend to the exterior bonnet locking pins from the larger grille, the mesh of which for the first time on a Mustang was a plastic moulding.

the herd that year; there was a broad, flat bonnet and sweeping roofline, combined with NASCAR-approved bonnet tie-downs and the 'Shaker' bonnet scoop. Under the aggressive looking bonnet was a 250bhp 351 V8, which gave the Mach I performance up in the Z/28 class, albeit with a few extra cubic inches.

All Mustangs benefited in 1969 from a wider range of engine options. It cost only $39, for example, to order the beefier 250 cid Six with 155bhp. Ford greatly abetted six-cylinder smoothness this year with 'center percussion' (forward-located) engine mounts, but the 250 was a lively Six as well, and Competitions Manager Jacque Passino was optimistic about a really high-performance Six. 'We've been putting out Mustang Sixes kind of artificially since '64 to fill up production schedules when we couldn't get V8s', Passino commented. 'I think there is a real market for an

inexpensive hop-up kit for the 250.' Unfortunately, said kit never materialized, nor did the fuel-injection six Passino wanted Ford to build. The 250 does remain susceptible to backyard hopping up, however, and is an intriguing and different way to build performance while retaining reasonable fuel mileage.

The base Mustang V8 in 1969 was a 302 cid engine with 220bhp, and the top-line V8 was the Cobra Jet 428, available with or without Ram-Air injection. The Mach I 351 engine was also available in other models, indeed almost every other Ford car except the Falcon. Though derived from the 289/302, the 351 was really a new engine. Its deck height was greater and its combustion chamber design different from the earlier small-blocks, and it was quite a bit heavier than the 302. But for all-out performance the mighty Cobra Jet was king, and with this engine the Mach I was

The concave front-end profile is clearly evident in this view of a 1969 Mach I. The functional bonnet air scoop was nicknamed the 'Shaker' because of its vibration at high rpm.

Two new performance models, the Boss 302 and the Boss 429, were added to the Mustang range for 1969. This is the Boss 429 engine installation in a car which was to be homologated for NASCAR racing. The work, which involved suspension alterations, was carried out for Ford by Kar Kraft in their Michigan workshops.

The fast lines of the 1969 Mach I are emphasized in this action shot by the slim body stripe running backwards from the front wheel well and incorporating italic lettering.

High-back seats were a feature confined to the Mach I in 1969 as a standard feature, but optional on most other models.

one of the world's fastest cars.

The Cobra Jet had been developed by the Light Vehicle Powertrain Department under Tom Feaheney. For the Mach I, it was combined with a tuned suspension engineered by Matt Donner, who employed 1967 heavy-duty suspension, but mounted one rear shock absorber ahead of the rear axle line and the other behind. The idea was to eliminate wheel judder on hard acceleration, and it worked. There was now a production Mustang that handled on the street like a Trans-Am racing car on the track. The 428 was still an enormous engine in this package, but with Donner's suspension the oversteer was readily controllable via the accelerator pedal.

'The first Cobra Jets we built were strictly for drag racing', Feaheney said. 'The '69s had a type of the competition suspension we offered in '67. Wheel hop was damped out by staggering the rear shocks. It was not a new idea, but it worked. Another thing was the (Goodyear) Polyglas tyre. I really can't say enough about this... In '69 every wide-oval tyre we offered featured Polyglas construction.' Combined with fine handling the Cobra Jet Mach Is naturally offered superb straight-line performance – the standing-start quarter-mile took about 13.5 seconds, pretty quick indeed for a four-seat automobile, even at the height of the muscle car era.

Shinoda's hand showed early in the Boss 302, released in early 1969 to compete with the Camaro Z/28 in the SCCA Trans-Am Challenge. Ford had to homologate 1,000 copies, but an actual total of 1,934 were built. In spite of its low production, the Boss brought people into showrooms, often to depart clutching order slips for milder-mannered Mustangs. Bunkie Knudsen knew what turned folks on.

To the Boss 302, Shinoda added front and rear spoilers which were effective at speeds over 40mph. The 4in-wide front spoiler was angled forwards to divert air away from underneath the car. The rear spoiler was an adjustable, inverted airfoil. Matt black rear window slats, like those of the Lamborghini Miura, did nothing to enhance airflow, but looked terrific. The aerodynamic gains resulted in a reduction of about 2½ seconds per lap at Riverside with no increase in engine power – but, of course, there *was* an increase in engine power, and a big one.

The Boss 302 was ostensibly pegged at 290bhp at 4,600rpm, but true bhp was as high as 400. There was good reason for this; the

The Grande in its production guise. The wire wheel trims and the contrasting colour of the top were part of the standard specification.

The interior of the Grande hardtop with teakwood grained trim and hopsack cloth and vinyl seats. Extra sound insulation was also provided.

Aggressive front of the 1970 Boss 302, Mustang's answer to the Camaro Z/28 and the Firebird Trans-Am. Although the engine was nominally rated at 290bhp, estimates ran as high as 400bhp.

The new grille emblem for 1970 combined the galloping horse with a red, white and blue tricolour, similar to that used on wings of early models. The wider grille and revised arrangement of lights offered a more unified appearance.

engine featured Cleveland heads with oversize intake valves and huge 1.75in exhaust valves inclined in enormous ports. There was an aluminium high-rise manifold, Holley four-barrel carburettor, dual-point ignition, solid lifters, bolted central main bearings, forged crankshaft and special pistons.

The Boss 302 came with ultra-stiff spring rates, staggered shocks, a stout Cobra Jet four-speed gearbox, 11.3in power front disc brakes, heavy-duty rear drum brakes and F60 x 15 Goodyear Polyglas tyres. To help prolong engine life, Ford fitted an ignition cut-out which interrupted current flow from coil to spark plugs between 5,800 and 6,000rpm, encouraging the driver to shift. Ford hadn't missed a trick; even the wheel wells were radiused to accept extra-wide racing tyres. On the street, the Boss 302 was unmistakable, with matt black centre bonnet section and grille extensions plus unique striping with 'Boss 302' lettering. For 1969, this was the ultimate Mustang.

Knudsen and his colleagues learned a fair amount from the new model variations. For instance, it seemed apparent that the luxury

The luggage compartment of a 1970 hardtop. The vinyl-covered infill panel between the lamp clusters identifies this as a Grande.

Engine compartments of Mustangs tend to be rather crowded places, especially when there is a V8 installed. This example dates from 1970, when the choice was between 302, 351 and 428 cid capacities.

field was far less important to Mustang than the performance area. Of 184,000 cars delivered in the first half of 1969, close to 46,000 were Mach Is, while only about 15,000 were Grandes. Division General Manager John Naughton accordingly promised 'heavy emphasis on performance' for 1970: 'We're going to be where the action is, and we're going to have the hardware to meet the action requirements of buyers everywhere.' The Boss 302, and the even hairier 1970 Boss 429, would go to the outer fringes of the market and the Trans-Am racing teams. But two Boss styling features – backlight louvres and adjustable rear spoiler – had such an impact that they were offered for any SportsRoof (fastback) Mustang.

Motor Trend agreed that the 1970 Boss was 'even Bossier' than it had been the year before. Unique side paint striping identified it, a well-engineered suspension was underneath, and its engine line-up was wilder than ever. New was a Hurst competition shifter with T-handle shift knob – the first Hurst linkage offered by Ford in a production Mustang. Further up the price scale at $4,000 was the promised Boss 429, fitted with Ford's Cobra Jet NASCAR racing engine: cast-magnesium rocker arm covers, semi-hemispherical combustion chambers, valves set across from each other for a crossflow head, enormous ports and intake passages and huge oval dual exhausts. It was a devastating performer, certainly the greatest Mustang Ford had ever built, and taking into account all the history since, it probably still leads the pack.

Mach I engines for 1970 ranged from the 351-inch two-barrel V8 up to the 428 four-barrel with Ram-Air. The Cleveland engine was further improved by canted-valve cylinder heads and larger intake and exhaust ports; extra durability was built into the block and rods. A rear stabilizer bar helped the car stick better in the corners while allowing the use of moderate spring rates to provide a reasonable ride. The 1970 Mach I was identified by a special grille fitted with driving lamps; 1969's dull-finish black centre bonnet

The 1970 dashboard remained virtually unchanged from the previous year's Mustang layout. As the car has no tachometer, the second of the large dials carries a combined fuel and temperature gauge.

High-backed seats were part of the standard equipment of SportsRoof models in 1970. That year the grille ornament was brought back to the centre of the car.

Highly decorative wheel covers were by no means the most attractive feature of the 1970 Mustang Grande, which continued to be offered with hardtop bodywork only.

Styling changes on the Grande for 1970 included a standard three-quarter landau-style vinyl-covered roof as well as vinyl inserts for the aluminium rocker panel mouldings. A full-length vinyl roof covering was an extra-cost option.

A mixture of houndstooth cloth and vinyl seat covering was offered for the Grande in 1970. Woodgrain trim was to be found on the dashboard, doors and even on the deluxe two-spoke steering wheel.

A low-angle view of the prototype 1970 Grande with the wire spoke wheel covers which had been familiar on the previous year's model. The dummy air scoops behind the door were to be eliminated from the production version.

section, twin racing mirrors, pop-open petrol cap and black honeycomb rear panel appliqué were continued.

The Grande was still offered with either Six or V8 engines; like all 1970 models it featured Mach I-style high-back front bucket seats, but unique were its landau-style black or white vinyl roof, twin racing rear-view mirrors, special identification and bright wheel lip mouldings. There were also very standard Mustangs at the bottom of the line, with Six or 302 V8 engines in the old trio of hardtop, convertible and fastback body styles. They featured new front-end styling and reverted to single headlamps and recessed taillamps. Inflation wasn't much of a factor in those days, and the six-cylinder coupe listed at only a shade over $2,700, while a V8 convertible could be had for just over $3,100. Convertibles, however, were fast disappearing; production was only 7,700 in 1970. Buyer preferences for closed models and air conditioning had reduced their popularity considerably.

Ford Division had gone all-out to put new life into the Mustang, and they may be credited for it. But they were also bucking a trend against the ponycar in general. Production in 1970 slipped by 100,000 units; fastbacks were down 40 per cent, hardtops 35 per cent. While the Mach I continued to account for a solid share of fastback sales, it was not a volume model and could not make up for competition by other products within and without the Ford Motor Company. The Boss 302 was strictly a limited-production car (6,318 for 1970). All signs pointed again to a serious product review in 1971 – particularly after Bunkie Knudsen had vanished as quickly as he had come.

Like Lee Iacocca after him and his own father long before, Knudsen was summarily dismissed. 'Things just didn't work out', said Henry Ford II, who is famous for his brief explanations. Industry observers suggested that Knudsen had accumulated too much power for his own good, and when an executive gets to such a level, his days at Ford are numbered. The respected Bob Irvin wrote: 'Knudsen moved in and started doing things his way. He was almost running the company and [some said] he had alienated many other top executives. Others said Knudsen's departure was

This is a 1970 Grande with the optional full-length vinyl top. Grandes in this form are more rare than those with the landau top, but all 1970 models are scarce as only 13,581 Grandes were built.

A frontal view of the Grande which reveals clearly the outline of the raised 'air splitter' pressing of the bonnet and the shallow fin effect along the top of the wings.

The 1970 Mustang in SportsRoof form. The air scoops outboard of the headlamps were non-functional.

The simple wheel trims identify this as a base model Mustang with SportsRoof fastback bodywork. Engine options started with the 200 cid Six, for which 120 bhp was claimed.

an indication of how the Fords don't like to share power.'

But now it was Lee Iacocca's hour at Ford, and to his credit, that hour would last far longer than Knudsen's. In place of Bunkie, HF2 announced that three Presidents would run Ford: R.L. Stevenson at International Operations, R.J. Hampson for Non-Automotive Operations, and Iacocca for North American Operations. In this triumvirate, North American Operations naturally dominated, and before 1970 was out the father of the Mustang had

become overall President of Ford.

The 1971 models were Knudsen's cars far more than Iacocca's. Indeed, it could be said that Iacocca was the force behind the dramatic shift in 1974 which saw the smaller Mustang II replace the 'original ponycar'. In the Mustang story, the 1971-73s exist as a sort of comma, between the heyday of performance and the new wave of sporty-but-economical Mustangs that Iacocca was to bring in.

The removal of the dummy air scoops from the panel ahead of the rear wheels helped to give the 1970 hardtop a smoother profile than its 1969 counterpart. The interior trim of the very long doors consisted of a one-piece moulding with a dummy wood insert.

Grabber was a new name to enter the Mustang vocabulary in 1970, standing in this instance for a decorated upmarket SportsRoof with C-stripes along the body sides and wheels with recessed hubcaps and bold chromed trim rings.

The mighty Cobra Jet 428 powered this 1970 fastback Mach I. The car's tuned suspension, designed by Matt Donner, featured one rear shock absorber mounted ahead of the rear axle and the other behind it. It was a successful attempt to eliminate wheel hop during hard acceleration.

1970 Mach I interior featuring deluxe three-spoke Rim Blow steering wheel, which operates the horn when depressed anywhere on its rim. The padded rim cover fitted here was intended to give extra grip. Above, the Shaker air scoop protrudes through the bonnet of a Mach I.

The impressive Boss 429 V8 put this 1970 Mustang at the top end of the performance scale with 375bhp on tap.

CHAPTER 9

Mustangs 1971 to 1973

Longer still, wider and lower

Given the three-year design lead time of Detroit, the 1971 Mustang was the answer to a question that nobody asked. It was designed in 1968-69, when the ponycar was still in its salad days, and built, furthermore, without sure knowledge of what the US Government would require in the middle 'Seventies. But no-one thought about an oil crisis, so it was natural to think about making the Mustang larger, rather than more economical. The biggest problem it seemed to have was space – for the back seat and in the boot. A long bonnet/short boot shape almost has to have these drawbacks, but a larger version also has to offer more space in every direction. Size, space and weight were accordingly the formula for 1971-73.

The influence of Ford's competitions experience under Knudsen was nevertheless evident in the '71 Mustangs. When they were designed, no-one could predict that Ford would get out of racing only six months after they appeared. That's why the sweeping, almost-horizontal roofline of the Ford GT showed up on the 1971 Mustang SportsRoof. The full-width grille scoops and rear deck scoops of the Shelby GTs were also picked up by designers. Available for 1971 were colour-co-ordinated polyurethane front bumpers, which helped the stylists shape a more interesting and better integrated front end. Larry Shinoda accompanied Bunkie Knudsen in departure from Ford in 1969 – but not before he had styled the '71. Thus the '71 is more pure-Shinoda than any other vintage, and many collectors praise its beautiful surface development, acute windscreen angle, hidden wipers and exotically styled cockpit.

The '71 was equally the most radical change in the cars since they had first appeared – fully restyled and as big as any Mustang would ever be. The wheelbase had only increased by an inch, but the car was 8in longer, 6in wider and close to 600lb heavier than the 1965 model. Though the familiar ponycar proportions were still there, the '71 was a more 'styled' car than any of its forebears.

Because more stringent emissions standards took effect in 1971, the number of Mustang engines was reduced for the first time in years. The Boss 302 was replaced by the Boss 351 Cleveland engine with four-barrel carb, 11:1 compression and 330bhp (gross) at 5,400rpm. The Boss 351 was more tractable than the Boss 302, and since it didn't rev as high, more durable. On other Mustangs, the standard 302 V8 with two-barrel carb and 9:1 compression gave 220bhp (gross) at 4,600rpm. The six was standardized 250 cid and 145bhp. The only other optional V8s were a four-barrel 302 (285bhp) and a four-barrel 429 (370bhp).

Mach Is equipped with the Cobra Jet 429 engine could be ordered with air conditioning ($407) and automatic transmission ($238), which were rather contradictions in terms; so were options like power steering, tilt steering wheel and 'sports deck' rear seat. Special Mach I options included a sports interior, power front disc brakes, centre console and special instrument group. Liberal use of the option book could raise the price of a Mach I from its $3,268 base to well over $5,000. Standard Mach I equipment included high-back bucket seats, integrated front spoiler, honeycomb grille, dual exhausts, auxiliary lamps and racing-style exterior mirrors. The 429 Cobra Jet engine cost $436.

The 429 CJ was still, emission controls and all, an astonishing engine. Mach Is so equipped would do 0-60mph in 6.5 seconds, 0-75 in about 9.0 seconds and the standing-start quarter-mile in 14.5 seconds. With the automatic transmission and 3.25:1 final-drive ratio they could reach 115mph and return the expected 10-11mpg. 'It is a decent mixture for those who want good perfor-

The 1971 Mustang line continued to evolve from the three basic models of convertible, notchback and SportsRoof fastback. The most changed models since 1965 were 8in longer and 6in wider than their predecessors, though only 1in was gained in wheelbase.

mance and some comfort', wrote Chuck Koch in *Motor Trend*, 'but it still remains a little unwieldy for city traffic.'

The Boss 351 Koch tested handled better than the Mach I because it had the competition suspension as standard – independent coil springs and hydraulic shocks up front, staggered rear shocks and front and rear stablizer bars. The test car did 0-60mph in 5.5 seconds and a 13.8-second quarter-mile, but with its rear axle ratio of 4.91:1 it would reach only about 100mph.

The 302 V8 with 220bhp was no match for these very powerful models (0-60mph in 10 seconds, a quarter-mile in 17.5), and its top

Up front the 1971 Mustang was the cleanest model yet, with a simple black mesh grille containing once again the original large-format galloping pony.

For 1971 the SportsRoof models featured a unique flat roof design and all-new sheet metal throughout. Rear three-quarter visibility was definitely not one of the car's strong points.

Redesigned rear light clusters and a black transverse strip carrying the Mustang name beneath the lip of the rear bodywork were identification features of this 1971 SportsRoof.

Bright mouldings along the body sides, on the rocker panels and around the wheel wells were standard on 1971 Grandes and optional on other models, including this SportsRoof. Recessed door handles were a 1971 safety feature.

The abbreviated vinyl covering of the roof of the 1971 Grande finished well above the baseline of the roof extensions flanking the recessed rear screen.

speed with the 2.79:1 ratio and automatic was only 86mph. But it was a good combination of power and economy, and probably the most flexible all-purpose powerplant for 1971.

The 1971 Mustang wasn't a bad car, but it certainly was the wrong car. By the time it came along the ponycar market had shrunk, and those who formerly flocked to Ford showrooms to see the new Mustangs were looking for something with more room. They didn't care much about fuel economy, because at that time petrol sold for 30¢ (about 15p today) per gallon, and long lines at filling stations were still two years into the future. As a car, it was really quite good, riding and handling better than its predecessors. The optional variable-ratio power steering gave it better road feel despite gains in weight and size; the low fastback design was lovely to look at in a year when the opposition didn't offer very much to

get excited about. The '71 lost few sales to Camaro, Firebird and Barracuda, but it was very definitely losing out to cars like the Maverick, Valiant and Nova, while the performance Mach I/Boss models remained a peripheral sideshow. The result was a production total of fewer than 150,000 units, with hardtops leading fastbacks four to three and convertibles accounting for only 6,000 sales.

In Detroit, one can do little with a one-year-old design but live with it (although there have been exceptions – Chevrolet's one-year run of 1958s comes to mind; however, this was dropped for reasons other than managerial dissatisfaction). Ford thus offered the same engine line-up in 1972, except for the Boss 351, which vanished. To meet the lower emissions requirements, the standard six and all V8s were detuned, and horsepower was now expressed

The 1971 Grande with its bright metal trim contrasting strongly with the car's dark paintwork. These wheel covers were standard equipment on the Grande and optional on other models. Over 17,000 Grandes were built in 1971 as the ponycar market turned increasingly towards luxury rather than performance.

Interior of the 1971 Grande, featuring cloth and vinyl high-backed seats, wood grain inserts and, almost inevitably, automatic transmission.

The Mach I was visually much changed for 1971. Bold treatment of the rocker panels and lower parts of the doors gave an impression of extra length to the already long bodywork. Automatic transmission and air conditioning became options, even when the 429 CJ engine was fitted.

Despite the fact that the big-block V8 would propel a Mach I from 0-60mph in 6.5 seconds, the car had a quieter appearance than in previous years, although this optional bonnet with NACA air scoops breathed performance.

This is the Mach I version of the substantially changed Mustang dashboard for 1971.

Recessed screen wipers—an important new Mustang feature for 1971—contributed to the clean lines of the Mach I's high-tailed bodywork.

The printed circuit rear screen defroster element can be clearly seen in this view of a 1971 Grande.

This is one of the prototypes of the 1971 Mustang convertible, featuring a non-standard hood. The car also went into production with a smooth-topped bonnet rather than with the NACA-ducted version seen here.

in nett, not gross figures. The 250 six was 98bhp, the 302 V8 110, and the standard 351s from 162 to 223bhp. Sales dropped again, this time by 20 per cent, though the convertible maintained its precarious level of 500 sales per month.

Ford was reduced in 1972 to promoting new colours and fabrics, one of the nicest being the Sprint decor option, available for closed models only. It could be combined with mag wheels, raised white-letter tyres and competition suspension. Sprints were usually painted white with broad, American racing blue strips edged with red. Complementary colours were used inside. But this, too, was a holding action; Iacocca now had the Mustang II well into the development stage. 'The Mustang market never left us', he said – 'We left it.' In a way he was right – the Mustang II was a lot closer to the original concept than the 1971-73 generation, and it sold in fabulous quantities.

The Mustang II was now just a year away, and for that year Iacocca reluctantly rode the 'original ponycar' into history. Actu-ally, sales improved this time, convertibles scoring double the number of units than in 1971 and 1972 – possibly because Ford made no secret that they were to be the last. Meanwhile, the Federal Government had issued impact standards for bumpers that would now have to sustain low-speed front and rear shunts without damage. Ford designed some pretty terrible looking cow-catchers, possibly out of dogged insistence that politicians are fools, an argument that always has partial validity. The Mustang's was probably the best of the Dearborn bumper brigade, jutting out only a bit more than in 1972. It consisted of an I-beam mounting bar inside a box-section bracket. This assembly was attached to two longitudinal rubber blocks which gave way on contact, then bounced back to their original position. An optional colour-keyed rubber cover was available to clean up their appearance.

The influences of other Federal requirements was evident throughout the '73. The dashboard was restyled to eliminate sharp controls and projections and it received extra padding. Larger

There were virtually no changes visible between the Mustang hardtop of 1972 and its counterpart of the previous year and the overall product range was cut down considerably by the deletion of various options.

The six-cylinder engine continued to be offered as the base Mustang engine, although as throughout Mustang history V8s continued to be the more popular option. This car is a pre-production example.

The 1972 convertible, an example of an increasingly rare breed, which received a more luxurious interior with additional woodgrain trim and improved vinyl-finished seats.

A 1972 convertible on test. This high-performance version has the optional bonnet top with the engine designation carried just behind the NACA intakes.

brakes, flame-retardant materials with a 'burn rate' of 4in per minute maximum and crankcase ventilation/exhaust gas recirculation were all part of the spec. The EGR system routed gases from the exhaust manifold through a vacuum valve into the carburettor, where they were diluted by the incoming fuel-air mixture. This permitted a leaner carb setting, hence lower emissions. Isn't that exciting?

Except for the front bumper, the '73 was little changed from 1971-72, and Mustang was the only Ford car to feature an optional 351 High-Output engine. Prices had been cut to help bump up sales in 1972, and they remained fairly stable. The base six-cylinder hardtop listed at $2,760, the V8 convertible was $3,189. The Mach I, which came with the 351 V8 and 162 nett bhp, sold for $3,088.

Nine years after the great debut, Mustang's old marketing technique of a wide range of options was still important. The '73 was 'designed to be designed by you', as Ford put it. The optional vinyl roof covering came in six colours and could be fitted to the

An attractive Sprint deco option was available for both hardtop and SportsRoof models, offering white with Shelby blue trim on the exterior and complementary upholstery inside. Mag wheels could also be ordered. This is one of the most desirable 1972s.

The 1972 Grande on display and on test. The vinyl roof continued to be a standard distinguishing feature, along with colour-keyed racing mirrors, distinctive wheel covers and a deluxe interior. The base price was under $3,000.

Despite many body changes, in 1972 the basic Mustang hardtop retained the long-bonnet, short-deck look made so famous seven years before. Hardtops continued to dominate sales, accounting for over 57,000 in 1972.

The last of the convertibles, in 1973, brought an upsurge in sales, with close to 12,000 built. Ford had announced that there was to be no topless model amongst the all-new Mustang II planned for 1974. The black bonnet finish was an optional extra.

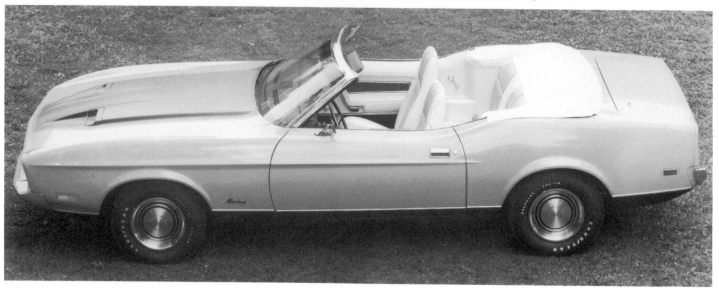

For 1973 the Mach I appeared with new body side and rear tape treatment and in common with other models featured a redesigned grille layout. The car on the right is fitted with the optional forged aluminium wheels.

whole roof on hardtops or the front three-quarters on fastbacks. Bonnets with lock pins and matt silver or black-coloured centre sections were available. Also on the list were forged aluminium wheels, 'metallic glow' paint and decorative striping. Convertibles and hardtops could be had with black-finish grilles which contained auxiliary driving lamps, and an electric rear window demister was available on closed cars.

The original ponycar went out on this note, and with it ends the collector story, as far as Mustangs are concerned, for the present and probably the distant future. There is virtually no interest in Mustang IIs, and the current 'third generation' cars, though much better, are too young to assess. Although all the 1965 to 1973 models are of a type, the Mustang had really evolved a long way in those years, becoming in the process something entirely different from that which Iacocca had originally intended for it. Press, public and Ford all knew this by 1973. But they were also aware of history. Rarely in the industry has a single model of any marque carried the impact of the Mustang, and those of us who love cars will be talking about it and restoring surviving examples for many years to come.

Last of the first-generation hardtops, the basic six-cylinder model had a list price of only $2,760 in 1973, a remarkable feat given the level of inflation over the previous seven years. It still represented excellent value.

Like all other 1973 Mustangs, the Grande carried a modified design of grille incorporating a rectangular mesh behind a new high-powered moulded urethane front bumper. Once again a vinyl top was a standard Grande feature.

CHAPTER 10

Mustangs in competition

From B-Production to Trans-Am and Europe

Mustang competition began and ended with Carroll Shelby. The whole purpose of Shelby's programme (see Chapter 7) was to create a genuine dual-purpose race-and-ride sports car out of the basic Ford package, and the idea worked. The Shelby GT-350 dominated its class in SCCA competition. Thanks to Shelby, Mustangs also made pretty fair showings in drag racing and in the Trans-Am Championship series.

The 'Competition Prepared' GT-350 was stripped of all insulation, carpeting, door panels and window operating mechanisms. The only glass it retained was the windshield. Plexiglas side windows in aluminium frames and a one-piece Plexiglas rear window were used for the rest of the greenhouse. A one-piece glassfibre front apron replaced the front bumper and gravel pan. The apron had a large cutout in its centre, which ducted air to the oil cooler, and two smaller holes for front brake cooling. The rear bumper, which on the first cars was painted white to match the body, was later left off entirely. A long-range 34-gallon gas tank was installed with a quick-release cap and a large splash tunnel. American Racing Equipment 7 x 15in five-spoke magnesium wheels were used exclusively on all racing GT-350s.

Even by racing standards, the interior of the competition model was stark. Almost everything was finished in semi-gloss black. The dash, from which all padding, the glove compartment, radio and ashtray had been removed, was left with only an ignition switch, light and wiper switches, and a bank of CS competition gauges. From left to right, they monitored fuel pressure, oil temperature, speed (0-160mph), revs (0-8,000rpm), oil pressure and water temperature. Two lightweight glassfibre racing bucket seats padded in black vinyl were used. There were also 3in competition

lap-belts, a rollbar and a fire extinguisher.

The 'R', or competition model, engines were advertised as fully dyno-tuned and race-ready. They developed between 325 and 350 gross horsepower. Beginning with the production 271bhp Hi-Performance 289 engine, Shelby balanced and blueprinted all components. Ports were enlarged, polished and matched to the combustion chambers. Pistons were fly-cut and a special camshaft was installed. A high-volume oil pump, oil cooler, special tube headers backed by straight pipes, and special valve cover breathers were fitted. The racing carburettor was a 715 cu ft/min Holley, which gulped air through a spun-aluminium plenum chamber mated to the hood scoop. The gearbox was Borg-Warner's T-10 Sebring model, supplied with both aluminium and cast-iron cases. A steel-plate competition clutch disc was fitted. Every R-model GT-350 was track-tested at Willow Springs Raceway prior to shipment.

The R-model listed for $5,950, a bargain price even for 1965. That, of course, was part of the Ford philosophy. Since 1962, the company had emphasized competition in an attempt to add a performance image to its street machines.

Not only did the image-making work, but the racing package itself was formidable. On Valentine's Day, 1965, Shelby American served notice that the only time Corvettes would see Victory Circle was when there were no GT-350s entered. Duly certified for Class B-Production in SCCA, the Mustangs went rapidly to work. The GT-350's first appearance resulted in three class wins.

Shelby Mustang dominance of B-Production wasn't quite universal, however. In 1965, when the SCCA awarded National Championships on a Divisional basis, one 327-engine Corvette eked out a win in the Southwest Region. The rest of 1965 – and all of 1966 and 1967 – was a Shelby Mustang parade. Here are the statistics:

B-Production National Champions

1965	Central:	Robert Johnson, GT-350
	Midwest:	Brad Brooker, Kansas, Corvette/GT-350
	Northeast:	Mark Donohue, New Jersey, GT-350
	Pacific:	Jerry Titus, California, GT-350
	Southeast:	Bill Floyd, South Carolina, GT-350
	Southwest:	Zoltan Petrany, Texas, Corvette
1966	Walter Hane, Florida, GT-350	
1967	Fred Van Buren, Mexico City, GT-350	

Another lesser-known Shelby Mustang effort was the drag racing programme in the National Hot Rod Association (NHRA). During May 1965, some members of the GT-350 project began exploring the possibilities of campaigning a GT-350 in NHRA B-Sports Production races. An earlier Shelby effort, the Dragonsnake AC Cobra, had put that car in the public eye on drag strips across the country. It seemed logical that a properly set up GT-350 could do the same thing for the Mustang.

The first GT-350 drag car was consigned to the noted engine and racing car builder Bill Stroppe for evaluation and development. NHRA had approved the engine modifications deemed necessary – machine-ported cylinder heads, 1.63in exhaust and 1.88in intake valves, heavy-duty valve springs, drag headers and complete balancing and blueprinting. But it was decided that Shelby's customer cars would be sold with the stock 306bhp engine. Full-tilt competition engines would be used for the factory cars and would be available to private owners as an option. Making the stock engine standard, Shelby decided, offered two advantages. First, the car could be sold at a lower list price; second, it would avoid creating hard feelings in any customer should he blow up an expensive full-specification factory-built engine.

The National Hot Rod Association approved a scattershield for the GT-350, placed in the trunk (mandatory because the car had solid lifters). A drag clutch and pressure plate were also certified. Approval meant that these parts could be installed and sold on the car as it left the factory, saving owners the time and expense of removing the engine or transmission to fit these parts later.

Other modifications developed as the Mustang drag racer took

shape. Cure Ride 90/10 up-lock shock absorbers were installed on the front, while Gabriel 50/50 down-lock shocks were used at the rear. Stroppe designed a set of ladder-bar torque arms. Also used was a Hurst Competition Plus shifter. Stroppe checked every loophole in the NHRA and AHRA (American Hot Rod Association) regulations. Some of his proposed modifications didn't make it to the strip because they were deemed not legal. These included lengthened front spindles, modified seat tracks, reradiused rear wheels and relocated front upper control arms. Stroppe even considered a Weber carburettor-equipped, roller-cam Factory Experimental model, but it never got past the bench-test stage.

The first drag racing GT-350 was completed and sold to a Shelby dealer in Lorain, Ohio, in August 1965. A second car was bought and run by Mel Burns Ford, of Long Beach, California. The actual number of GT-350 drag cars is not known. In addition to the 1965 models, a few 1966s were similarly prepared.

Overshadowed by the GT-350's stunning success in SCCA club racing was the Trans-Am effort. Trans-Am is short for the Trans-American Sedan Championship, first run in 1966. Essentially, it was an offshoot the SCCA's sedan (saloon) class events. The Trans-Am attracted Mustangs, Barracudas, Falcons, Dodge Darts and a host of under-2-litre cars. Trans-Am races were intended to be 'mini-enduros' that ranged anywhere from 200 to 2,400 miles, or two to 24 hours, and thus required pit stops for fuel and tyres. By the end of 1966, Trans-Am racing was one of the most popular series on the SCCA schedule, and many professional factory teams had entered. To make things more interesting, a Manufacturer's Trophy was offered to the maker whose cars won the most races. Driver ego took a back seat as each factory vied with its rivals to uphold its performance image.

Trans-Am rules were based on FIA Appendix J specifications for Series Production Cars (Group 1) or Touring Cars (Group 2). These cars were limited to engine displacements between 2,000 and 5,000cc, a maximum wheelbase of 115in and minimal performance modifications. Since only four-seaters were allowed, the GT-350 could not be used because it was officially a two-seat car. In its place, the Mustang notchback hardtop was pressed into service.

The 1966 schedule had seven races, but the winner wasn't decided until the last race at Riverside, California – the series was that close all season. But it was at Riverside that a huge blue Shelby

A Shelby Mustang GT350 leads the rolling start of an SCCA race at Elkhart Lake's Road America circuit in Wisconsin, with a Corvette alongside it, as another Shelby car and a younger Corvette lead the pursuit from the second row.

American race van appeared with a Shelby-ized notchback Mustang for Jerry Titus, Editor of *Sports Car Graphic* and a former GT-350 team driver. Titus took the pole position in qualifying laps and ultimately won the race, which gave the Manufacturer's Trophy to Ford for 1966.

The eleventh-hour appearance of Shelby American signalled a change in Ford racing priorities, probably because everyone realized that the 1967 GT-350 would not be as competitive as the older R-models. The factory's Trans-Am effort would now have to be carried out with Mustang notchbacks.

Earlier in the season, Shelby American had permitted Mustang sedan competitors to participate in its race-assistance programme because the notchbacks shared virtually all mechanical components with the GT-350s. This offer of support was later withdrawn because it was felt that there was not enough product identification between the Shelbys and the stock notchback sedans. Ford took up the slack by offering limited factory support to outstanding teams, but by the end of the season both Ford and Shelby American were committed to Trans-Am.

Not wanting to let its 1966 championship seem like a fluke,

Ford sponsored a fully-fledged two-car victory team put together by Shelby American. The canary yellow Mustang notchbacks with flat black hoods ran under the banner of Terlingua Racing Team, an honorary team composed of sponsors of Shelby's Terlingua (Texas) Boys' Ranch.

The 1967 Trans-Am saw other factory teams running new-model ponycars. A team of racing Cougars was fielded by stock car ace Bud Moore. Camaros, prepared by Roger Penske, were piloted by former GT driver Mark Donohue. Other well-known drivers in 1967 were Dan Gurney, Parnelli Jones, George Follmer, Peter Revson, David Pearson, Ronnie Bucknum and Jerry Titus, and the season was extended to 13 races. Shelby American's Mustang notchback crossed the finish lines often enough to pick up the trophy for a second year. Interestingly, most of Ford's attention that season was paid to the Bud Moore Cougars. They received more financial consideration than other Ford teams, plus 'trick' parts and drivers of the calibre of Gurney and Jones, but despite that, Shelby American came home first.

By 1968, Group 2 rules were becoming difficult to manage, so they were bent slightly. All engines were allowed to be bored out to a limit of 5 litres (306 cubic inches). A minimum weight of 2,800lb was set, and wheel rims up to 8in wide could be used. The schedule again included 13 races. Shelby's Mustangs and Penske's Camaros were joined by a pair of factory-backed AMC Javelins, while the Cougars bowed out.

The 1968 Shelby Trans-Am racers were painted blue or red with flat black bonnets, and ran under the Shelby Racing Company banner. Titus, still the lead Shelby driver, finished first in the initial 24-hour event at Daytona, but by the second race the Penske/Donohue Camaro team had started to click. They won the next

Mustangs in competition were by no means confined to the United States. Here is the Swedish driver Bo Ljungfeld about to win his class in the Rangiers hill-climb in Switzerland at the wheel of a Mustang prepared in Britain by Alan Mann.

Parnelli Jones and his Mustang with Mark Donohue's Javelin close behind lap a slower moving Camaro during a Trans-Am race at Mosport, Ontario, in 1970. Mustangs were to win six of the 11 qualifying races that year to pick up their third Trans-Am title.

eight races before Titus broke the string at Watkins Glen, but by that time there was no catching the Camaro, and it went on to take the 1968 Championship.

By the first race of 1969, rules for Trans-Am cars differed even more from those governing Group 2 cars. Mustang fastbacks were now legal and the new Boss 302 was the hot ticket. Shelby's team prepared a pair of these to compete in the 12-race schedule; they

were to be driven by Peter Revson and Horst Kwech. A second Boss 302 team, fielded by Bud Moore, had Parnelli Jones and George Follmer in the driver's seats. Massive factory engineering efforts now produced semi-tube-frame chassis (thinly disguised as roll-cages), acid-dipped bodies, huge tyres, flared fenders, spoilers, wings and mind-boggling horsepower. The Boss 302 canted-valve engine made an impressive debut in the first race of the season, and after a post-race check of lap charts, Parnelli Jones' Bud Moore Mustang was declared the winner.

The second race, at Lime Rock, Connecticut was won by Sam Posey in a Shelby-prepared Boss 302. That was the Shelby team's only victory that year, and at Riverside, on October 4, 1969, Carroll Shelby announced his retirement from racing.

Trans-Am racing reached its peak during the 1970 season. Despite the absence of the Shelby team, there were at least a half-dozen other big league entries: Penske Javelins, Bud Moore Boss 302 Mustangs, Jim Hall's Chaparral Camaros, Jerry Titus' Firebirds, Dan Gurney's Barracudas and Dodge Challengers and the Owens/Corning Camaros. The Mustang was Trans-Am Champion once again in 1970, beating all its impressive rivals.

After 1970, the factories began to withdraw their support, possibly because they had created an overwhelming amount of competition. In place of the factory teams, more and more independents began to enter, but as they quickly learned, the price of being competitive was astronomical. Also, Detroit's ponycars had begun to increase in size and weight, and foreign names like Porsche, Alfa Romeo and Datsun had started to win races regularly. In a desperate attempt to attract the large crowds of 1970, SCCA allowed A-Production, B-Production and A-Sedan cars to compete in the 1971 Trans-Am series, which meant Corvettes, Camaros, Datsun Zs – even Cobras and GT350s. But the electricity and excitement of earlier seasons had all but disappeared. The Trans-Am had come and gone, at least for the time being, but the Mustang and Shelby American had been an exciting part of it.

Who says motor sport is not truly international? This is Frank Gardner and his Mustang leading the oversteering Camaro of fellow Australian Brian Muir as they dominate a touring car race in England.

Gardner versus Muir again, only this time Muir's Z/28 holds a slight lead over Gardner's Boss 302 in the Guards Trophy race at Brands Hatch in 1970. Note the front and rear spoilers added to the Mustang as part of the race preparation by Motor Racing Research Ltd.

Gardner saves precious inches as he holds his Boss Mustang on the tightest possible line through Druids Hairpin at Brands Hatch.

Mustangs and other American-built heavy racing metal may have been in the minority in British saloon events of the late 'Sixties and early 'Seventies, but what they lacked in numbers they made up for in drama. Here a Mustang lays rubber at Silverstone as a gaggle of Escorts, Minis and Imps begin their forlorn chase.

Buying a Mustang

Model identification and collector preferences

When buying a Mustang, the first rule of thumb is to be sure the car is authentic. It is also the second and the third rule. There is an important difference in value between a Mustang that is genuinely to original specification, with only the appropriate options, and one which has been equipped with non-authorized options and purports to be something other than what it started life as being. Expertise and experience are all important when it comes to in-depth model identification, which is why Greg Wells, a foremost Mustang authority, has been asked to compile the words which follow . . .

As the 20th anniversary of the Mustang's introduction approaches it is appropriate to ask just why this car is so popular with collectors. Certainly the same factors of styling, sportiness and mechanical simplicity appeal to the car collector of today as strongly as they did to the new car buyer of 1965 and beyond. Cars are collected for their nostalgic powers, too, and the Mustang is used by many to stimulate the memories of a simpler, more pleasant time.

In addition to these reasons, the Mustang's unparalleled adaptability, a major factor in its runaway sales success when new, continues to provide a 'car for all seasons' for the latter-day enthusiast. Whether it is an 'econo-Stang', a 'power-Pony', or a 'luxury-horse' one desires, the almost infinitely variable Mustang could and continues to provide it. The miles-long option and accessory list which allowed the Mustang to be customized to the buyer's liking broadened its markets enormously and accounts for the vast variety of Mustangs available to the collector.

The happiest situation for the Mustang collector has to be the fantastically good parts availability. In the last decade, hundreds of vendors and suppliers have begun reproducing and stocking virtually all of the parts necessary to restore any Mustang. While it is true that parts are still a problem for certain models, the Boss 302 and 429 for example, many of the difficult-to-restore items are now available again. Reproduction upholstery, both Pony and regular interiors, is now available from a number of sources. Emblems, stainless trim, wiring, replacement body panels, etc, are all available, too. With the possible exceptions of VWs, no other car enjoys such a great supply situation for its restorers. In fact, the availability of parts for 1965-73 Mustangs probably surpasses that of many new cars!

The Mustang is the fourth great collector car from the drawingboards of the Ford Motor Company and as such follows in the treadmarks of its illustrious predecessors: the Model T, the Model A and the *en-bloc* V8. Its popularity and longevity on the collector car scene seem destined to outstrip all of the others due to the Mustang's supreme usability. Few other collector cars, Ford or not, can offer the continued economy, enjoyment and utility embodied in the Mustang. Whether daily driver or trailer-pampered show car, there is little doubt that the 21st century will see the Mustang's popularity unabated among collectors everywhere.

In the following sections, we will attempt to delineate the better buys and the most desirable models of each year. In addition, we will mention various things to look for when buying an early model, what to be concerned about and what to ignore, which are good buys and which to avoid.

1964½-1965

All first-year Mustangs are considered by the factory, and coded on the data plates, as 1965 models. Officially, Ford never referred to any of the cars as '1964' or '1964½'. However, just as with the Models T and A, many changes were made to the car during the first months of production, and among collectors the easiest way to differentiate between the early production vehicles and the later ones is to term the first cars '1964½'. The factory never did this in the sales literature of the time, but the service side did and the collectors have picked up the designation for their own use. Some of the differences between the early and late cars are an alternator instead of a direct-current generator, a non-adjustable passenger seat on the early cars, differing spare tyre hold-down brackets and myriad other minor details which occurred as Ford fine-tuned their design to allow the high production levels needed to supply the unprecedented demand. In general, the earlier cars are more desirable than the later ones. Certainly, a 1964½ Mustang is more difficult to restore accurately than a later 1965 car.

Important options to consider when assessing the relative worth of a particular Mustang are the performance-oriented ones. 'Total Performance' was the slogan during much of the Mustang's life, and performance options are among the more desirable. Certainly,

the most sought-after option is the 271bhp-rated High Performance 289 cid V8, known to collectors as the 'Hi-Po'. This engine featured special big-valve heads, cast-iron exhaust headers and a mechanical cam, and was not available until June 1964. Only a few thousand buyers opted for this $276 option ($328 when purchased along with the GT Equipment Group) and this fact, combined with the hard usage most Hi-Pos received at the hands of their hot-rod owners and drivers, has made the true Hi-Po Mustang a rare steed indeed. Collectors refer to these cars as 'K cars', not from any Chrysler comparisons, but due to the data plate code for the Hi-Po engine. If one is looking at a Hi-Po Mustang, it is very important that the car is a true Hi-Po in both engine and data plate. In a high percentage of the time, actual K-serial cars will be missing the Hi-Po engine or will have a non Hi-Po 289 dressed up with the Hi-Po cosmetic equipment.

Another option which is desirable is the GT Equipment Group, an appearance and handling package which consisted of dual grille-mounted foglights, expanded instrumentation (the so-called five-dial dash), the Special Handling Package (increased-rate front and rear springs, larger front and rear shock absorbers, a 22.1:1

Here is a basic 1965 Mustang fastback as you might find one today, sadly in need of bodywork and a new interior, but in sound running order.

steering ratio and a larger diameter front stabilizer bar), a dual exhaust system with bright trumpet extensions, front disc brakes, GT rocker panel stripes and other GT ornamentation. The GT Equipment Group was not available at production start-up, but was introduced to coincide with the car's anniversary of introduction during April 1965. As is the case with the Hi-Po engine, one must look very carefully at any Mustang purported to be a GT. Two emblems and exhaust trumpets do not a GT make! Since all of the components of the GT Equipment Group were available separately, both over-the-counter and on the order blank, one must check for completeness when looking at a possible GT pony. The GT package was available only in combination with the 225bhp and 271bhp engines.

Other options that collectors seek include power steering and power brakes (especially important options on V8-equipped cars), air conditioner (a hump-mounted hang-on unit; a built-in unit was not available until 1967), styled steel wheels and Cruise-O-Matic three-speed automatic transmission. Consoles and AM/8-track radios are also desirable.

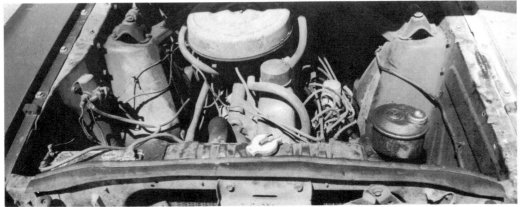

This fastback Six was restored as a project by the editors of *Consumer Guide,* who kindly loaned the author the photographs which appear in this chapter, as well as many which are reproduced elsewhere. The six-cylinder cars are being chosen by many collectors these days because of their economy, relative ease of repair and reasonable performance, although V8s continue to excite most Mustang enthusiasts.

Trim being removed from the Mustang's rear deck. Most of the work here is ordinary unbolt stuff, but everything removable has to come off before working on the body.

Dents are hammered out using a support on the opposite side of the sheet metal. The remaining dents must then be filled and sanded smooth.

Ample adjustment is possible to ensure a perfect fit of Mustang doors. Here, the worst body damage has already been repaired and sanded smooth. Primer is then applied to the bare metal areas preparatory to the initial coat of the finish paint.

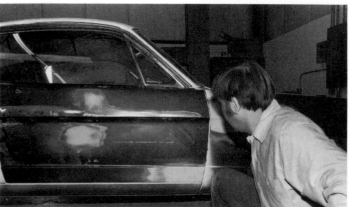

A strong aftermarket in Mustang accessories and supplies helps to make restoration painless, if not inexpensive. This vinyl seat kit is being installed on an old frame which has been stripped and repadded with new foam. Exact match of upholstery type and colour is essential in any restoration.

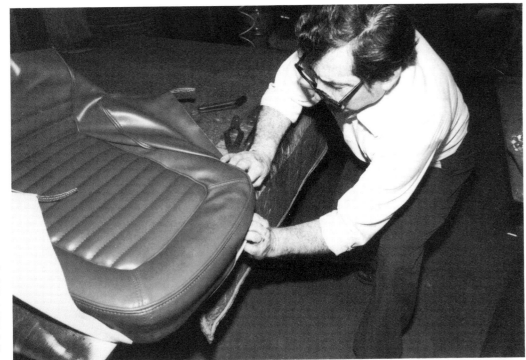

New door panels, also available as 'new old stock' or reproduction, are fitted to the doors after the surrounding exposed metal sections have been resprayed. Steam cleaning the engine compartment can be a messy business, but is essential before attending to individual engine components which may require repainting.

1966

Only minor differences exist between the late 1965 cars and the 1966 units. As one collector explains: 'There are more real differences between the 1964½ cars and the 1965s than between the 1965s and the 1966s'. Therefore, most of the information in the preceding section applies to the 1966 cars as well.

One change for 1966 was the availability of a specially strengthened Cruise-O-Matic with the 271bhp Hi-Po 289 (previously only the four-speed was available with this engine). Automatic transmission installation percentages were very high in the Mustang, with only 14.5 per cent of buyers opting for the four-speed in 1965, dropping to 7.1 per cent in 1966. Interestingly, collectors seem to prefer the automatic over the four-speed, too, except for certain of the performance-oriented models.

An important option which was introduced during mid-1965 was the Interior Decor Group. This is commonly referred to as the 'Pony' interior because of a panel carrying embossed horses as decoration. The Decor Group package consists of unique seat and decor panel upholstery, woodgrain trim on the dash panel and glove box door, a simulated walnut grain steering wheel and door handles, partially carpeted under-dash kick panels, bright trim on the foot pedals and door-mounted red and white courtesy lights. The Interior Decor Group was available on all Mustang body styles and is indicated on the data plate by a 'B' after the body style code. Standard interior cars carry an 'A' suffix on the body style code. Again it must be emphasized that the car's equipment should match the data code's indicated equipment, or a reduction in valuation is in order.

Other significant options include a power top on the convertible models, limited-slip differential, the Visibility Group (remote-control door mirror, day/night mirror, two-speed electric wipers), the Rally-Pac (a steering column pod containing a clock and a tachometer) and the extremely rare AM/FM radio option, which is also seen on a few late 1965 Mustangs. This last option can easily bring $1,000 or more. Among a small cadre of Mustang collectors, the six-cylinder, four-speed transmission is a sought-after combination. This model used the so-called Dagenham four-speed transmission from the European parts bins. Six-cylinder sales were up this year, to an installation percentage of 41.7, the only year that the V8's fitment percentage did not increase over the previous year. However, the six-cylinder, four-speed combination is

relatively rare; the majority were allied to the automatic.

As well as considering options on a particular car, the prospective Mustang buyer must be concerned with the condition of any car inspected. The major problem with Mustangs, as is true with almost every collector car, is that of rust. The Mustang's unitized platform-type frame is fairly susceptible to the ravages of metal cancer and one must inspect carefully to determine to what extent the disease has been allowed to progress. Areas to look at include the cowl vents, just in front of the windshield, the bottoms of the doors, floor pan areas, the trunk floor, frame rails, all seams where the unibody is welded together, shock towers, the engine bay, etc. Doors that do not shut or align well are usually warning signs of rust elsewhere in the body. Happily, most panels are now available to repair serious rust, but this type of repair is very expensive to do well. The top dollar and the most desirable car is the one with little or no rust. Unfortunately, a totally rust-free Mustang is very, very hard to find.

1967

This is the year of the Mustang's first major restyle, and also marks the availability of several new options for the line. For the first time, the big-block 390 cid Thunderbird Special became available in the Mustang. This engine was rated at 320bhp. Other new options for the 1967 line included a fingertip speed control (cruise control), a $71 option; a Tilt-Away steering wheel; and a Competition Handling Package. This last was available only in concert with the GT Equipment Group and consisted of a limited-slip differential and a minimum final drive ratio of 3.25:1. This is a rare option to find today and would add considerable value to a car so equipped.

Increased competition from other manufacturers contributed to a decrease in Mustang production in 1967, a fact also influenced by the restyling which, while retaining the Mustang family characteristics, was not as crisp and appealing as the original 1965-66 design to most buyers (and collectors). This is reflected in the 10-20 per cent higher value collectors place on the 1965-66 cars *vis-a-vis* the 1967 vehicles, all other factors being equal. For the purposes of driving, a case can be made for the 1967 car over the first models as Ford incorporated a number of improvements to the '67 based on field experiences with the earlier cars.

A few other 1967 options deserve mention. One is the Exterior Decor Group, which consisted of hood vents with integral turn signal indicators, bright trim around the wheel wells and a pop-open gas cap. On the 2+2, this option included a ribbed aluminium trim panel insert in the rear valance panel between the tail lights. Another option is the new-style SelectAire air conditioning, which is a built-in unit, for the first time in the Mustang (hang-on under-dash units were still available as a dealer-installed option). A third option worth mention is the Convenience Control Panel, which was available with air conditioning only in concert with a console. This was a set of four warning lights covering the parking brake, door ajar, seat belt reminder and low fuel warning. Convertible buyers were given the option to purchase a folding glass rear window in place of the all-too-easily discoloured standard plastic rear window.

In summary, the 1967 Mustang option list was even longer than before and allowed the buyer incredible flexibility in tailoring a Mustang to his or her wishes. Many of the options new to the list were comfort or convenience items and these were an omen of the direction the Mustang would take in following years. The rough and ready pony would be transformed into a well-mannered horse; performance would still be a factor, but luxury and comfort would become the sales tools of emphasis.

1968

Externally, 1968 Mustangs differed little from the preceding year. Virtually the only exterior key to the 1968 pony is the presence of side marker lights as required by new US regulations concerning automotive safety and design. A number of other not-so-obvious changes were made to the 1968 car to comply with these new regulations, especially in the interior. Most obvious of these was a new padded steering wheel. One drawback to the 1968 interior, as compared to the 1967 and earlier cars, is a greater use of mylar chrome (aluminized plastic brightwork giving the impression of polished metal trim). This material is one of the first to deteriorate in the interior and one of the most difficult to restore. Only recently have Mustang parts vendors mastered processes that can attack this problem. However, it can be expensive and many times is not as attractive as assembly-line-fresh components. In general, the later the

Mustang the more plastic to be found in the interior construction, and the more difficult and expensive is the interior restoration.

Powertrain availability for the 1968 car was expanded. Initially, the 200 cid six-cylinder was the base engine, with the 289 cid 2V, the 289 cid 4V and the 289 cid 4V Hi-Po optional. Soon after introduction, both the 289 4V and the 289 Hi-Po were dropped to make room for a new 302 cid 4V rated at 230bhp. During mid-year, the 289 2V was deleted and a 302 2V of 220bhp added. Two high-performance engines were offered to replace the highly-missed 289 Hi-Po: a 302 High Performance and a 390bhp 427 big block. Both of these engines are extremely rare and would command top figures on the block. In November 1967, the 250 cid six-cylinder previously used as a truck engine was added to the option list; in January 1968, the new 428 cid 4V Cobra Jet became available. This last engine was very much underrated at 335bhp, probably in an attempt to secure a more favourable rating from competition sanctioning bodies and insurance companies. The Cobra Jet is very, very rare and is worth perhaps twice as much as a base six-cylinder with three-speed transmission.

The year 1968 reaffirmed Mustang's shift towards luxury and comfort. Fully 71.8 per cent were ordered with automatic transmission and 51.8 per cent with power steering. Six-cylinder engines were no longer available with anything but the automatic transmission, and the four-speed installation dropped to a mere 6.1 per cent of cars sold. In an interesting aside, the 427 was available only with a beefed-up Cruise-O-Matic.

In comparison to the 1965-66 models, the 1967-68 vehicles (which can conveniently be considered together) are worth perhaps 10-20 per cent less than the corresponding earlier models similarly equipped.

1969

As the horsepower race heated up among producers of the ponycar genre, Ford took a different approach to the marketing of Mustang options. In place of offering individual and package options, Ford began offering different models which were essentially Mustangs with different option packages as standard. For example, the Grande was a luxury-oriented version of the hardtop. The Mach I was essentially a performance version of the new SportsRoof, a term Ford adopted in 1969 for the fastback body style. Also new for 1969 were two ultra-high-performance models, the Boss 302 and the Boss 429.

In terms of desirability, these two new Bosses are the most sought-after cars of this year. The Boss 302 was produced to provide Ford with a homologated model to enter in the Sports Car Club of America's production-based Trans-Am racing series, and as such is probably the peakiest, least compromised of the performance-oriented Mustangs ever offered. Certainly, the Boss 302 was the best handling Mustang ever offered by Ford. The Boss 429 was a vehicle used to homologate the awesome Boss 429 'Semi-Hemi' for NASCAR oval-track use. Although providing incredible straight-line performance, the Boss 429 was something of a freak in nature, considerably too heavy in the front end to handle very well. The 429 is the most expensive 1969 Mustang to buy today, but the supply of these cars in good or better condition is very surprising. It seems that most Boss 429s were driven very little; in fact, these cars were viewed as collectibles almost from the day of their introduction. On the other hand, the Boss 302 was viewed as a potent street killer and many of these cars were run into the ground. The 302 car is worth perhaps half of the Boss 429's value, but is a much harder car to find in excellent condition, either restored or not.

Other performance-oriented options available that year included the Cobra Jet 428 engine, which could be ordered with a Ram-Air cold-air induction system, and the GT Equipment Group. The GT package was included with the Mach I model, which accounted for approximately 25 per cent of Mustang production that year. The GT option by itself (not as part of the Mach I package) is rare and therefore commands a premium over the standard car almost equal to the increase one would allow for a Mach I.

Engine availability for 1969 changed little from the late-year line-up of 1968. The list for 1969, in order of descending desirability, is as follows: the 428 cid 4V 335 bhp Cobra Jet V8 with Ram-Air, the 428 4V 335bhp V8, the 390 4V 320bhp V8, the 351 4V 290bhp V8, the 351 2V 250bhp V8, the 302 2V 220bhp V8, and the 250 1V 155bhp six-cylinder. The Mach I carried the 351 2V as standard equipment. The Boss 429 came

with two different versions of the Semi-Hemi, an 'S' version, which was the heavy-duty variant and worth 5-10 per cent more than the milder 'T' series engine.

There was a confusing array of interior decor packages available which will not be delineated as most were available only on lower-level models beneath the Mach I and Grande, as these two vehicles carried most of the upper-level trim anyway. Other significant interior options were high-back front bucket seats, a power ventilation system (not available with SelectAire air conditioning), an intermittent windshield wiper system and a Rim-Blow steering wheel. This last is something of a liability since it has a tendency to actuate under the driver's grip during spirited cornering.

In comparison with the 1967-68 cars, the 1969 is considered by most collectors to be a more handsome design and, as such, 1969 (and 1970) values tend to be a little higher, especially for the Mach I and Grande models. The 1969-70 years represent the zenith of the performance car in Detroit and in Dearborn. Increasing federal intervention in the automotive design area, as well as increasing outcry from insurance companies over accident rates for the (usually young) drivers of performance vehicles would conspire to remove performance from the auto manufacturer's sales tools. In following years the lithe, sleek Mustang would become heavier and bigger and more and more oriented to the older, more affluent buyer, who wanted the performance image only.

1970

As indicated in the previous section, the 1970 line can be considered along with the 1969 cars. There were few styling changes of any consequence, the major one being a shift to two headlamps from the four carried by the 1969 cars. The GT Equipment Group was not available for 1970, although the enthusiast could select a competition suspension on lower-level cars; it was included on the Mach I, Boss 302 and 429, and whenever the 428s were specified. Another very interesting performance-oriented option was the Drag Pack, which was available only with the 428 V8s with 3.91 or 4.30:1 rear axle ratios. This consisted of a strengthened rotating assembly, stronger connecting rods, and a heavy-duty oil cooler, and was intended for the buyer who wished to drag race his Mustang.

This package would be worth an additional 10-15 per cent over the otherwise standard 428 pony.

Appearance options of note included an odd array of vinyl top treatments, including a blue and green houndstooth pattern and a leather-look Saddle Kiwi design featuring Western trim. Either of these two options in good condition is rare today and virtually unrestorable if in poor shape. They would increase a car's worth some 5-10 per cent. The rear window slats which had been a feature of the 1969 Boss 302 were now available on any SportsRoof fastback and proved to be a popular fitment; add 5 per cent to any Mustang so equipped. Other appearance options which would affect value are Magnum 500 wheels (on a Boss 302 only) or styled steel wheels.

Engine options for 1970 follow along from the 1969 list, except that the big-block 390 was dropped. In the case of the Boss 429, the 820T engine was now joined by an 820A engine, and it is indicative of the direction in which the Mustang emphasis was headed to note that the main difference between the two engines had to do with a modified emission control arrangement on the 'A' mill. Mustang for 1971 would move substantially away from the performance arena, much more so than in any previous year.

1971

Mustang for 1971 was easily recognizable as a totally different car, for it grew in every dimension except for height. Most Mustang styling cues were retained, although much of the new look was taken from the Shelby Mustangs of 1969-70. The new Mustang was also a considerably heavier car than its predecessors. The changes must have been at odds with Mustang buyer wishes, as sales, which had been dropping every year since 1966, plummeted to nearly a third of their 1965-66 yearly rates. Clearly, this new, bigger, heavier Mustang was not as appealing to buyers.

Model line-up for 1971 was similar to the previous year: hardtop, SportsRoof fastback, convertible, plus the 'package cars' of Mach 1 and Grande. The Boss 302 and 429 were dropped, to be replaced by a Boss 351 of very limited production.

Powertrain availability was greater than in the immediate past. The base engine for most models was the 250 cid 145bhp six-cylinder. The Mach I base engine was the 302 2V 210bhp V8. Four 351s were available: a 2V 240bhp unit, a 4V 285bhp version, an HO version for the Boss 351 boasting 330bhp, and a late-year 4V 351 Cobra Jet entry with an advertised 280bhp. A 429 cid engine replaced the 428 previously used. This was not the same engine as used in the Boss 429, but was rather a development of the 390 FE 'Thunderbird Special' engine first used in 1967. The 429 was rated at 370bhp with or without the optional Ram-Air induction. Also available was a 429 Cobra Jet, offered with the Drag Pack option; this was termed 'Super Cobra Jet' in some advertising and literature.

Installation percentages for options and accessories for 1971 confirm the overwhelming shift to comfort and convenience. Fully 90.2 per cent of 1971 Mustangs were ordered with V8s, with 83.9 per cent of all cars carrying the automatic transmission. Power brakes came on 40.9 per cent, power steering on 85.7 per cent and air conditioniong on 40.5 per cent. Vinyl tops were fitted to 29 per cent of 1971 Mustangs. This was the last year that the fingertip speed control was available on the Mustang, and the first year in which power windows could be ordered; a mere 1.9 per cent of 1971 Mustangs were so fitted.

The most desirable of the 1971 models to today's collector would have to be the 1971 Boss 351. This last of the Boss cars was not available when the 1971 line-up was introduced in August 1970, but was first shown in late November of that year. The Boss 351 featured a standard 3.91:1 Traction-Lok rear axle, a four-speed transmission with Hurst linkage, and a quick 15.7:1 steering ratio.

Unfortunately, the 1971 models were bloated all out of proportion styling-wise, in comparison to the 1965-66 and the 1969-70 cars. Whereas in the past a Mustang had to earn its stripes, beginning in 1971, Ford stylists slathered racing-looking stripes over any Mustang model that would benefit from the treatment. The last straw was the availability of the Boss 351 stripe package on the standard hardtop model. This alone certainly would not account for the low sales volume of the Boss 351, but it didn't help at all.

1972

Reflecting the Mustang buyer's chagrin over the behemoth now carrying the name, Mustang sales continued to decline in 1972.

The last token performance model of any real strength was gone, as were all of the 429 engines. Ironically, the wish to make the 429 available in the Mustang is one of the major reasons the car grew in size for 1971. Engine availability for 1972 was now down to just five: the 250 cid six-cylinder (the base engine for all models save the Mach I), the 302 2V V8, the 351 2V V8, the 351 4V V8 and a new 351 4V HO. All 1972 engines would run on low-octane regular fuel and no official power output values were quoted. Ford seemed more proud of the fact that unburned hydrocarbon emissions had been reduced by more than 85 per cent and carbon monoxide emissions by almost 60 per cent. Little wonder that performance took a second seat during those days.

In hopes of reviving the sagging sales picture, Ford unveiled two special models termed Sprints. These were primarily trim packages featuring red, white and blue exterior finishes with USA emblems, and colour-keyed interior and exterior trim. The unfortunate part of the '72½ Sprint Decor Option is that a similar package was offered on the lowly Pinto, with which the Mustang was seen grouped during much of the advertising of the Sprint package. For today's collector, the Sprint package is probably desirable (and worth about 15 per cent more than a comparable car). It should be noted that there were really two Sprint Decor Groups available for the 1972 car; the more collectible one included Magnum 500 wheels and F60 x 15 raised-white-letter tyres. The lesser Sprint package omitted the wheels and tyres and is worth only an additional 10 per cent over the base car.

It must have been obvious to the Ford Motor Company's movers and shakers that the 1971-72 Mustang was not going to do the job. For the 1972 model year, Mustang production was only 119,920; compare this to 1965's model year production of 499,242 or 1966's 547,512. This was simply an insufficient number of cars to allow a respectable level of profitability. Therefore, a new, smaller Mustang was in the works, a reversion to the original concept of a secretary's car, rather than what amounted to a smaller Torino. Sales for Mustang for 1973 would increase only slightly, but by then many knew the '73 Mustang would be the last of the original line.

1973

The 1973 Mustangs are slightly more desirable than their immediate predecessors, a result of the 'last of the breed' syndrome. In point of fact, there is very little difference between the 1971, 1972, or 1973 cars. The telling visual indicator for the 1973 models was a revised grille treatment with vertical parking lamps inset. In addition, the taillamp panel was changed noticeably. The single model of the 1973 line-up that gathered most of the attention for the year was the convertible. Ford had already announced that the new Mustang to be introduced for 1974 would not feature a convertible amongst the body styles available. Therefore, a veritable gold rush for last-year Mustang convertibles warmed the cockles of many a dealer's cold heart.

Ford offered another new way to package options for the 1973 year. These were the basic equipment package. Package A was comprised of the Cruise-O-Matic, power steering and power front disc brakes, AM radio and whitewall tyres. The B package added air conditioning, tinted glass and a full-length console to the contents of package A.

Models available for 1973 were essentially only three: hardtop, SportsRoof and convertible. Engines options were equally limited. These were the 250 1V six-cylinder, the 302 2V V8, the 351 2V with or without Ram-Air, and a 351 4V. It is probably sufficient testimony about Ford's performance intentions to note that only on the last engine was a four-speed even available.

One new-for-1973 option (one wonders why they even bothered!) was a deluxe leather-wrapped two-spoke steering wheel. One option change was the dropping of the Magnum 500 wheel, which had been available for many years. These were replaced on the option list by a five-hole slotted-dish wheel.

The Mustang had grown too fat, too big and too slow to suit most Mustang lovers. Of course, the car remained 'designed to be designed by you' and thus somewhat true to its original concept. But for the emission-strangled 'Seventies and beyond, a new Mustang would be required, one which harked back to the original's simple, light, moderate execution. The Mustang II was perhaps not exactly what the doctor ordered, but it was undoubtedly a step in the right direction.

APPENDIX A

Technical specifications

1965

Engines: Standard: 6-cyl, 3.5 x 2.95in, 170cid, CR 8.7:1 1v Autolite carb, 101bhp at 4,400rpm (April-September 1964); 6-cyl, 3.68 x 3.13in, 200cid, CR 8.7:1, 1v Autolite carb, 115bhp at 4,400rpm (September-on, previously optional). Optional: V8, 3.80 x 2.87in, 260cid, CR 8.8:1, 2v Autolite carb, 164bhp at 4,400 rpm (April-September 1964); V8, 4.00 x 2.87in, 289cid, CR 9.3:1, 2v Autolite carb, 200bhp at 4,400rpm (September-on); V8, CR 10.5:1, 4v Autolite carb, solid lifters, 271bhp at 6,000rpm (from June 1964).

Transmissions and rear axle: Standard; 3-speed manual all engines except 271bhp V8; Cruise-O-Matic optional except on 271bhp V8; 4-speed manual mandatory on 271bhp V8, optional on all others except 260cid V8. Rear axle ratios: 3.50:1 on 170 6-cyl; 3.20:1 on 200 6-cyl; 3.00:1 on 260 V8 and all Cruise-O-Matic V8s and 225bhp V8 with manual; 2.80:1 on 200bhp V8 with manual; 3.50:1 on 271bhp V8; 3.89:1 and 4.11:1 optional on 271bhp V8. Limited-slip differential available with 2.83/2.80/3.20:1 ratios and 3.00:1 ratio with 271bhp V8s.

Suspension and brakes: Ifs, coil springs, wishbones; live rear axle, semi-elliptic 4-leaf springs. Steering: recirculating ball, worm and nut, standard ratio 27:1, optional ratio (with power assist or Handling Package) 22:1. Brakes: hydraulic drums all round, power assist optional, power front disc brakes optional from late 1965. Tyres: 6.50 x 13 standard, 7.00 x 13 optional (std with Handling Package); 6.95 x 14 optional from September 1964 (std on V8s); 6.95 x 14 dual red band premium nylon optional on V8s from September 1964 (std on 271bhp V8); 5.90 x 15 optional with Handling Package April-September 1964. Pressed steel ventilated disc wheels with 5 studs (4 on 6-cyl), rims 4.5in (5.0in optional April-September 1964 V8s, standard from September onwards).

Dimensions: Wheelbase 108.0in; front track 56.0in (V8s), 55.4in (sixes), rear track 56.0in; length 181.6in; width 68.2in; height 51.5in; unladen weight of standard coupe 2,583lb, convertible 2,789lb, fastback 2,633lb. Basic price on introduction: coupe $2,372, convertible $2,614, fastback $2,589. (£1.00 = $2.80.)

1966

Engines: As per 1965 with 170cid 6-cyl and 260cid V8 not offered. For the 6-cyl 200cid engine: CR 9.2:1, 120bhp at 4,400rpm.

Transmissions and rear axle: As per 1965. Ford-Dagenham gearbox used as 4-speed option on 6-cyl; Cruise-O-Matic now optional for any engine.

Rear axle ratios: 3.20:1 std on 6-cyl manual, optional on Cruise-O-Matic; 2.83:1 std on Cruise-O-Matic 6-cyl; 2.80:1 std on 200bhp V8; 3.00:1 std on 225bhp V8; 3.50:1 std on 271bhp V8; 3.89:1 optional on 271bhp V8. Limited-slip differential available with all ratios except 3.89:1 and 3.20:1/Cruise-O-Matic.

Suspension and Brakes: As per 1965. Tyres: 6.95 x 14 rayon std, 6.95 x 14 nylon optional, 6.95 x 14 premium nylon optional (no-cost option with 271bhp V8). Blackwalls std, whitewalls optional, dual red bands on 271bhp. Ventilated pressed steel wheels with 5 studs (4 on sixes), rims 5.0in (4.5in on sixes).

Dimensions: As per 1965. Unladen weight of 6-cyl coupe 2,488lb, convertible 2,653lb, fastback 2,607lb. Basic price on introduction: coupe $2,416, convertible $2,653, fastback $2,607.

1967

Engines: As per 1966 with addition of optional V8: 4.05 x 3.78in, 390cid, CR 10.5:1 4v Holley carb, 320bhp at 4,600rpm.

Transmissions and rear axle: 3-speed manual std with 6-cyl and 200/225bhp V8s; 4-speed manual available with V8s only; Select-Shift Cruise-O-Matic optional on all engines; Heavy-Duty 3-speed manual optional on 390 V8. Rear axle ratios: 3.20 std on manual 6-cyl, optional on automatic; 2.83:1 std on automatic 6-cyl; 2.80:1 std on 200bhp V8s; 3.00:1 std on 225 and 320bhp V8s, optional on 200bhp V8s (mandatory with F70-14 Wide-Oval tyres; available only with limited-slip diff on 200bhp V8s with 3-speed manual); 3.50:1 std on 271bhp V8s; 3.25:1 with limited-slip diff optional on 320bhp V8; 3.89:1 optional on 271bhp V8. Limited-slip diff available with 3.00/3.25:1 ratios.

Suspension and brakes: As per 1966, with track widened 2½in front and rear; front suspension altered; 2½in longer lower wishbones; lower A-frames; separate cam adjustment for camber and castor; polyethylene-filled ball-joints. Manual steering ratio now 25.3:1. Dual master cylinder brake system introduced with power assist or power front discs optional. Tyres: 6.95 x 14 standard, 7.35 x 14 standard with 390 V8; other sizes available.

Dimensions: Wheelbase 108.0in; track 58.5in; length 183.6in; width 70.9in; height 52.0in; unladen weight of standard 6-cyl coupe 2,568lb, convertible 2,738lb, fastback 2,605lb. Basic price on introduction: coupe $2,461, convertible $2,698, fastback $2,592.

1968

Engines: Standard; 6-cyl, 3.68 x 3.13in, 200cid, CR 8.8:1, 1v Holley carb, 115bhp at 3,800rpm. Optional: 6-cyl, 3.68 x 3.91in, 250cid, CR 9.0:1, 1v Motorcraft carb, 155bhp at 4,000rpm (from November 1967); V8, 4.00 x 2.87in, 289cid, CR 8.7:1, 2v Holley carb, 195bhp at 4,600rpm; V8, 4.00 x 3.00in, 302cid, CR 9.0:1, 2v Motorcraft carb, 220bhp at 4,000rpm: V8, 302cid, CR 10.0:1, 4v Motorcraft carb, 230bhp at 4,800 rpm; V8, 4.05 x 3.78in, 390cid, CR 10.5:1, 4v Holley carb, 325bhp at 4,800rpm; V8, 4.23 x 3.78in, 427cid, CR 10.9:1, 4v Motorcraft carb, 390bhp at 4,600rpm; Cobra-Jet V8, 4.13 x 3.98in, 428cid, CR 10.7:1, 4v Holley carb, 335bhp at 5,600rpm (from January 1968).

Transmissions and rear axle: 3-speed manual std all engines except 390cid V8 (Heavy-Duty 3-speed), 427 V8 (Cruise-O-Matic) and 428 Cobra-Jet (4-speed or Cruise-O-Matic). 4-speed manual optional on 289 and 302 V8s. Select-Shift Cruise-O-Matic optional throughout. Rear axle ratios: 3.20:1 std on 6-cyl manual, optional with Cruise-O-Matic; 2.83:1 std on 6-cyl Cruise-O-Matic; 2.79:1 std on 289 V8, optional on 302 V8; 3.00:1 std on 302 V8 (limited-slip diff optional) and 390 V8, optional (with/without limited-slip diff) on 289 V8; 3.25:1 optional on 289 V8 and 390 V8 (mandatory when 390 fitted with air conditioning); 3.50:1 standard on 427/428 V8 (limited-slip diff available).

Suspension and brakes: As per 1967, with new curved lower arm struts, softer front bushings, precompressed strut insulator bushings for improved castor alignment.

Dimensions: As per 1967. Unladen weight of standard 6-cyl coupe 2,635lb, convertible 2,745lb, fastback 2,659lb. Basic price on introduction: coupe $2,602, convertible $2,814, fastback $2,712.

1969

Engines: Standard: As per 1968. Optional: 6-cyl, 250cid as per 1968; V8, 4.00 x 3.00in, 302cid, CR 9.5:1, 2v Motorcraft carb, 220bhp at 4,600rpm; V8, 4.00 x 3.50in, 351cid, CR 9.5:1, 2v Motorcraft carb, 250bhp at 4,600rpm; V8, 351cid, CR 10.7:1, 4v Motorcraft carb, 290bhp at 4,800rpm; V8, 4.05 x 3.78in, 390cid, CR 10.5:1, 4v Holley carb, 320bhp at 4,600rpm; Cobra-Jet V8, 4.13 x 3.98in, 428cid, CR 10.6:1, 4v Holley carb, 335bhp at 5,200rpm; Super Cobra-Jet V8, 428cid, CR 10.5:1, 4v Holley carb, 360bhp at 5,400rpm, Ram-Air induction.

Transmissions and rear axle: 3-speed manual std all engines with 200 to 351cid. 4-speed manual available on all V8s. Select-Shift Cruise-O-Matic available on all engines. Rear axle ratios: 3.08:1 std on 200cid manual 6-cyl, optional with auto; 2.83:1 std with 200cid auto 6-cyl; 2.79:1 std on 302 V8 with 3-speed or auto and 250cid 6-cyl with auto, optional on 250cid manual 6-cyl and 302 V8 with 4-speed; 3.00:1 std on 250cid 6-cyl manual, 302 V8 4-speed, 250bhp V8 4-speed, all 280bhp V8s, 390cid V8 4-speed, optional on 250cid auto, 302 V8 auto, 302 V8 3-speed and auto; 2.75:1 std on 250bhp V8 3-speed and auto, and 390 V8 auto; 3.25:1 std on non-Ram-Air 428 V8, optional on all 351cid V8s, all 390cid V8s and Ram-Air 428 V8; 3.50:1 std on Ram-Air 428 V8, optional on 250bhp 4-speed, all 390 V8s, all

non-Ram-Air 428 V8s; 3.91:1 optional on 280bhp V8 4-speed and all 428 V8s; 4.30:1 optional on 280bhp V8 4-speed, 390 V8 4-speed and all 428 V8s. Limited-slip differential available with 3.50/3.91/4.30:1 ratios.

Suspension and brakes: As per 1968. Wheel size increased to 14 x 6in on all cars equipped with 428 V8s. Tyres: C78 x 14 std on 6-cyl and 302 V8s; E78 x 14 std on 351/390 V8s, optional on 6-cyl and 302 V8s; E70-14 Wide-Oval Fibreglass belted whitewalls std on all GTs and non-Ram-Air 428 V8, optional on all 302/351/390 V8s; FR70-14 Wide-Oval radials optional on all V8s except Ram-Air 428; F70-14 Fibreglass belted mandatory on Ram-Air 428 V8.

Dimensions: Wheelbase and track as per 1968. Length 187.4in, width 71.3in, height 52.0in; unladen weight of standard 6-cyl coupe 2,798lb, convertible 2,908lb, fastback 2,822lb; Boss 302 fastback 2,822lb, Grande coupe 2,873lb, Mach I fastback 3,175lb. Basic price on introduction, coupe and fastback $2,635, convertible $2,849, Boss 302 $3,588, Grande $2,866, Mach I $3,139.

1970

Engines: Standard except Mach I/Boss 302: 6-cyl, 200cid, CR 8.0:1, 120bhp at 4,400rpm. Optional: 6-cyl, 250cid, CR 9.2:1, 150bhp at 4,000rpm; V8, 302cid, 220bhp and 290bhp with 4v Holley carb and 10.6:1 CR; V8, 351cid, Cleveland heads and canted valves, 250bhp at 4,600rpm with 2v Motorcraft carb and 9.5:1 CR or 300bhp (sometimes rated at 290bhp) at 5,400rpm with 4v Motorcraft carb and 11.0:1 CR, with or without Ram-Air (std Mach I); V8, 302cid, CR 10.6:1, 4v Holley carb, 290bhp at 5,800rpm (std Boss 302); Cobra-Jet V8, 428cid, CR 10.6:1, 335bhp at 5,200rpm; Super Cobra-Jet Ram-Air V8, 428cid, CR 10.5:1, 360bhp at 5,400rpm; V8, 4.36 x 3.59in, 429cid, CR 11.3:1, 4v Holley carb, 375bhp at 5,600rpm (std Boss 429).

Transmissions and rear axle: 3-speed manual std all engines with 200 to 351cid except Boss 302. 4-speed manual std Boss 302/429, optional other V8s; Select-Shift Cruise-O-Matic optional throughout except on Boss 302/429. Rear axle ratios: 3.08:1 std on manual 200cid 6-cyl, optional on auto; 2.83:1 std on auto 200cid 6-cyl; 2.79:1 std on auto 250cid 6-cyl, 220bhp/302 V8 3-speed and auto, 250 6-cyl 3-speed; 2.75:1 std on non-Ram-Air 351 V8 3-speed or auto, optional on Ram-Air 351/Mach I 3-speed and auto; 3.00:1 std on 220bhp/302 V8, 250cid 6-cyl auto, 250bhp/351 V8 4-speed, Ram-Air 351/Mach I V8 with 3-speed or auto, non-Ram-Air 351 with auto, optional on 250cid six auto, 220bhp/302 V8 3-speed or auto, 250bhp/351 V8 3-speed or auto, Ram-Air/Mach I 351 V8 4-speed, all 4v 351 V8s except non-Ram-Air auto, and 428 auto; 3.25:1 std on 300bhp/351 V8s except non-Ram-Air 300bhp, 250bhp/341 V8 4-speed and non-Ram-Air 428 V8, optional on all 250bhp/351 V8s except Ram-Air 4-speed, 428 Ram-Air 4-speed and auto, and 300bhp/351 non-Ram-Air auto; 3.50:1 std on Boss 302 and Ram-Air 428, optional on 300bhp/351 4-speed and auto, 428 non-Ram-Air; 3.91:1 std Boss 429, optional on Boss 302; 4.30:1 std on Boss 302. 3.00/3.25:1 ratios available with optional Traction-Lok diff, 3.91:1 ratio available with Traction-Lok (mandatory on Boss 302); 4.30:1 ratio available only with

Detroit Automotive No-Spin 'Locker' diff.
Suspension and brakes: As per 1969.
Dimensions: As per 1969 except width 71.7in; unladen weight of std 6-cyl coupe 2,822lb, convertible 2,932lb, fastback 2,845lb, Boss 302 fastback 3,227lb, Grande coupe 2,907lb, Mach I coupe 3,240lb. Basic price on introduction, coupe $2,721, convertible $3,025, fastback $2,771, Boss 302 $3,720, Grande $2,926, Mach I $3,271.

1971

Engines: 200cid 6-cyl engine deleted, 351 Windsor V8 replaced by smaller Cleveland 351 V8, 4v Boss 351 replaced Boss 302 early 1971. Standard except Mach I/Boss: 6-cyl, 250cid, CR 9.0:1, 1v Motorcraft carb, 145bhp at 4,000rpm. Optional: V8, 302cid, CR 9.0:1, 220bhp at 4,600rpm; V8, 351cid, CR 9.0:1, 250bhp at 4,600rpm; V8, Cleveland 351cid, CR 10.7:1, 285bhp at 5,400rpm; V8, 351cid, CR 11.1:1, 330bhp at 5,400rpm (std Boss 351); Cobra-Jet V8, 429cid, CR 11.3:1, 370bhp at 5,400rpm; Super Cobra-Jet Ram-Air V8, 429cid, CR 11.3:1, 375bhp at 5,600rpm. All 351 V8s available with Ram-Air induction.
Transmissions and rear axle: As per 1970. Rear axle ratios: 3.00:1 std on manual six, 250bhp/351 Ram-Air 3-speed and auto, 285bhp/351 non-Ram-Air auto, optional on six auto, 302 V8, 250bhp/351 V8; 2.79:1 std on six auto, 302 V8 auto and 3-speed; 2.75:1 std 250bhp/351 non-Ram-Air V8; 3.25:1 std on all 285bhp/351 V8s except non-Ram-Air auto and non-Ram-Air 429 V8s, optional on all 250bhp/351 V8s, 285bhp/351 auto V8; 3.50:1 std on Ram-Air 429 V8, optional on non-Ram-Air 429; 4.11:1 ratio offered only on special drag-pack. Traction-Lok differential available with most 3.00-3.91:1 ratios, Detroit Locker diff available with some high numerical ratios.
Suspension and brakes: As per 1969. Steering ratios: 30.2:1 manual, 22:1 power.
Dimensions: Wheelbase 109.0in. Front track 61.5in, rear track 61.0in, length 189.5in; width 74.1in; height of hardtop 50.8in, convertible 50.5in, SportsRoof fastback 50.1in; unladen weight of standard coupe 3,087lb, SportsRoof 3,057lb, convertible 3,209lb, Boss 351 3,281lb, Grande 3,049lb, Mach I 3,220lb. Basic price on introduction: coupe $2,911, SportsRoof $2,973, convertible $3,227, Boss 351 $4,124, Grande $3,117, Mach I $3,268.

1972

Engines: (ALL BHP RATINGS NOW SAE-NETT.) All 429 V8s deleted. Standard: 6-cyl, 250cid, CR 8.0:1, 98bhp at 3,400rpm. Optional: V8, 302cid, CR 8.5:1, 142bhp at 4,000rpm; Cleveland V8, 351cid, 163bhp at 3,800rpm with CR 8.6:1 and 2v Motorcraft carb, 200bhp with Ram-Air available; also 223bhp at 5,400rpm with CR 8.6:1 and 4v Holley carb; High-Output Cleveland V8, high-lift camshaft, mechanical lifters, forged aluminium pistons, shot-peened connecting rods, special intake manifold, 351cid, CR 8.6:1, 4v Autolite carb, 266bhp at 5,400rpm.
Transmissions and rear axle: As per 1971. Rear axle ratios: 3.00:1 std on 6-cyl 3-speed, 302 V8 3-speed and California auto, optional on 6-cyl auto

and 302 V8 auto; 2.75:1 std on 163bhp/351 non-Ram-Air V8 (mandatory with air conditioning); 2.79:1 std on 6-cyl auto and 49-state 302 V8 auto; 3.25:1 std on 163bhp/351 Ram-Air V8 and 248bhp/351 V8 (mandatory with air conditioning), optional on 163bhp/351 non-Ram-Air V8 4-speed; 3.50:1 std on 248bhp/351 V8, 3.91:1 std on 266bhp/351 V8 4-speed. Traction-Lok diff available with most ratios, Detroit Locker diff deleted.
Suspension and brakes: As per 1971.
Dimensions: As per 1971. Unladen weight of standard coupe 2,941lb, SportsRoof 2,909lb, convertible 3,061lb, Grande 2,965lb, Mach I 3,046lb. Basic price on introduction: coupe $2,729, SportsRoof $2,786, convertible $3,015, Grande $2,915, Mach I $3,053.

1973

Engines: As per 1972, with H-O 266bhp/351 deleted. Bhp ratings: 250cid six 99, 302 V8 136, 351 V8 163, 200 (223 with 4v). 6-cyl engine std all models except Mach I, on which 163bhp/351 V8 standard.
Transmissions and rear axle: 3-speed manual std on 6-cyl and 302 V8s, 4-speed manual optional on 253bhp V8s, Select-Shift Cruise-O-Matic optional on all models, mandatory on 163/200bhp V8s. Rear axle ratios: 2.79:1 std on 6-cyl and 302 V8 auto; 2.75:1 std on 163bhp/351 auto (mandatory with air conditioning); 3.00:1 std on 6-cyl and 302 V8 3-speed (mandatory on V8 with air conditioning), optional on 6-cyl and 302 V8 auto (mandatory with air conditioning); 3.25:1 std on 200/223bhp/351 V8 auto (mandatory with air conditioning), optional on 163bhp V8 with auto and 223bhp V8 with 4-speed (mandatory with air conditioning); 3.50:1 std on 223bhp V8s. Traction-Lok diff available with 3.00:1 ratio on 302 V8 and 6-cyl with 2.79:1 ratio on auto, 2.75:1 ratio on auto, 3.25:1 ratio on auto and 223bhp V8 4-speed, and with all 3.50:1 ratios.
Suspension and brakes: As per 1971-72, with front suspension given ¼in greater travel and longer shock absorbers. Larger front/rear drum brakes on standard hardtops and SportsRoof fastbacks, power front disc brakes standard on all convertibles. All wheels 5-lug. Steel-belted radial tyres offered for first time as Mustang options across-the board. 5mph bumpers added.
Dimensions: Front track 61.0in, rear track 60.8in; length 194.0in; height of hardtop 50.7in, SportsRoof 50.0in, convertible 50.4in; unladen weight of standard hardtop coupe 2,995lb, SportsRoof 3,008lb, convertible 3,126lb, Grande 3,003lb, Mach I 3,115lb. Basic price on introduction: coupe $2,760, SportsRoof $2,820, convertible $3,102, Grande $2,946, Mach I $3,088.

1965 Shelby GT-350 fastback

Engine: V8, 4.00 x 2.87in, 289cid, CR 10.0:1, 306bhp at 6,000rpm, equipped with high-riser aluminium manifold, centre pivot float four-barrel carb, tuned exhaust system, Cobra aluminium finned valve covers, extra capacity finned oil pan.
Transmission and rear axle: All-synchro Borg-Warner Sebring close-ratio four-speed manual gearbox with lightweight alloy case. Gear ratios: 2.36:1 first, 1.62:1 second, 1.20:1 third, 1:1 top. Rear axle ratio: 3.89:1.

Suspension and brakes: Computer designed geometry, 1in front anti-sway bar, torque-control stabilized-life rear axle with No-Spin differential, 15in wide-base steel wheels, Goodyear Hi-Performance Blue Dot tyres, Kelsey Hayes front disc brakes with competition pads, wide-drum rear brakes with metallic linings, Koni shocks.

Dimensions: Wheelbase 108in; track 57.0in front and rear, length 181.6in; width 68.2in; height 55.0in; unladen weight 2,800lb. Basic price on introduction $4,195, $4,547 with dealer preparation and Federal Excise Tax.

Factory rated performance: 0-60mph 5.7 secs, 0-100mph 14.9 secs, standing-start ¼-mile 14.5 secs at 98mph, top speed 133mph.

Competition version: As above plus: glassfibre front lower apron, engine oil cooler, large capacity radiator, brake cooling assemblies, 34-gallon (US) petrol tank, quick-fill fuel cap, electric fuel pump, large diameter exhaust pipes without muffler, 7 x 15in magnesium bolt-on wheels, altered wheel openings, roll-bar, shoulder harness, fire extinguisher, plastic rear window, aluminium-framed sliding plastic side windows, complete instrumentation including oil temp and fuel pressure. Dyno-tuned Shelby competition engine.

Drag version: GT-350 equipped with heater, seat-belts, drag headers, Cure-Ride 90-10 up-lock front shock absorbers, Koni rear shock absorbers, rear slicks, 4.86:1 rear axle ratio, rev counter, NHRA scatter-shield, Hurst shifter, carburettor plenum chamber, 15in wheels, tuned chassis. List price $5,041.

1966 Shelby GT-350 fastback (6 convertibles built specially)
Engine: As per 1965 with side-exit exhausts.

Transmission and rear axle: As per 1965 with Detroit Locker rear axle optional.

Suspension and brakes: Wheels: 14in Motor Wheel Magnum 500s replaced 1965's Cragar 15in magnesium wheels on option list in mid-model year. Also optional: 14in cast-aluminium 10-spoke wheels.

Dimensions: As per 1965. Basic price on introduction $4,428 plus prep and tax.

GT-350H: Special model built for leasing by Hertz Rent-a-Car, equipped with 14 x 6in Magnum 500 steel styled wheels with chrome lug nuts and special centre assemblies; 2 to 3-bolt master cylinder mounting bracket with 3-bolt Almico master cylinder; competition brake warning decal; Ford C4 automatic transmission, Ford 460 cu ft/min carburettor, gold side striping, Motorola AM radio.

1967 Shelby GT-350 fastback
Engine: As per 1965-66. Bhp approximately 290 through switch to stock Ford headers.

Transmission and rear axle: C4 automatic now optional. Rear axle ratios: 3.89:1 manual, 3.50:1 automatic.

Suspension and brakes: Wheels: 15 x 6½in pressed-steel, mag-style slotted hub caps standard; 15 x 7in Kelsey Hayes Mag Star 5-spoke chromed aluminium steel-centre wheels optional. Tyres: Goodyear Speedway 350.

Dimensions: As per 1967 Mustang. Basic price on introduction: $3,995.

1967 Shelby GT-500 fastback
Engine: V8 4.13 x 3.98in, 428cid, CR 10.5:1, 355bhp (actual bhp approx 400) at 5,400rpm. Shelby-modified with special high-rpm hydraulic valvetrain, high-lift camshaft, dual-point distributor, twin 4v Holley 600 cu ft/min carbs.

Transmission and rear axle: All-synchro close-ratio 4-speed manual or C6 automatic. Rear axle ratios: 3.50:1 manual, 3.25:1 automatic.

Suspension and brakes: As per 1967 GT-350.

Dimensions: As per 1967 Mustang. Unladen weight 3,000lb. Basic price on introduction $4,195.

1968 Shelby GT-350 fastback & convertible
Engine: V8, 4.00 x 3.00in, 302cid, CR 10.5:1, 4v Holley carb, 250bhp at 4,800rpm. Optional: supercharged 335bhp at 5,200rpm.

Transmission and rear axle: As per 1967 GT-350.

Suspension and brakes: Mustang heavy-duty suspension with special grommets and Shelby special front anti-roll bars, Blue Gabriele adjustable shock absorbers. Wheels: Ford 15in, mag-style 5-spoke hubcaps standard, 15 x 7in aluminium alloy 10-spoke wheels optional. Tyres: Goodyear Speedway raised white letter (some used Goodyear Polyglas blackwalls). Power-assisted steering and brakes mandatory options.

Dimensions: As per 1968 Mustang. Unladen weight of fastback 3,146lb, convertible 3,332lb. Basic price on introduction: fastback $4,117, convertible $4,238.

1968 Shelby GT-500 fastback & convertible
Engine: Standard: as per 1967 GT-500; Optional: V8, 4.23 x 3.78in, 427cid, CR 11.6:1, 4v Holley carb, advertised 400bhp at 5,600rpm.

Transmission and rear axle: As per 1967 GT-500.

Suspension and brakes: As per 1968 GT-350.

Dimensions: As per 1968 Mustang. Unladen weight of fastback 3,445lb, convertible 3,631lb. Basic price on introduction: fastback $4,317, convertible $4,439.

1968 Shelby GT-500KR fastback & convertible
Engine: V8, 4.13 x 3.78in, 428cid, 4v Holley 735cu ft/min carb, est 400bhp. Oil cooler fitted on air conditioned cars.

Transmission and rear axle: As per 1968 GT-500; when 4-speed was specified, rear shock absorbers staggered on either side of the rear axle to control axle hop. Rear axle ratio: 3.50:1 (Traction-Lok diff on non-air cond cars.)

Dimensions: As per 1968 Mustang. Unladen weight of fastback, 3,545lb, convertible 3,731lb. Basic price on introduction: fastback $4,473, convertible $4,594.

1969-70 Shelby GT-350 fastback & convertible
Engine: V8, 4.00 x 3.50in, 351cid, CR 10.7:1 4v Autolite carb, 290bhp at 4,800rpm.
Transmission and rear axle: Ford 4-speed top-loader all-synchro manual gearbox with 11in clutch plate standard, Ford C4 automatic optional. Rear axle ratios: 3.25:1 standard, 3.00/3.50:1 optional, Traction-Lok optional.
Suspension and brakes: Mustang heavy-duty suspension with Ford Adjust-O-Matic shock absorbers on export mountings. Brakes: 11.3in ventilated power disc front, heavy-duty drums rear. Power steering standard. Wheels: 15 x 7in mag-style 5-spoke with chromed-steel rims and cast-aluminium centres. Tyres: Goodyear belted E70 x 15 Wide-Oval standard, F60 x 15 optional, all with raised white letters. Some cars sold with Boss 302 steel wheels.

Dimensions: As per 1969-70 Mustang. Length: 190.4in. Unladen weight of fastback, 3,600lb, convertible 3,689lb. Basic price on introduction: fastback $4,434, convertible $4,753.

1969-70 Shelby GT-500 fastback & convertible
Engine: V8, 428cid, 335bhp at 5,200rpm.
Transmission and rear axle: 4-speed all-synchro close-ratio manual gearbox standard, Ford C6 automatic optional. Rear axle ratios: 3.50:1 standard, 3.91/4.30:1 optional, Traction-Lok diff optional.
Suspension and brakes: As per 1969-70 GT-350.
Dimensions: As per 1969-70 Mustang. Length: 190.4in. Unladen weight of fastback 3,850lb, convertible 3,939lb. Basic price on introduction: fastback '$4,709, convertible $5,027.

APPENDIX B

Production figures and engine options

Mustang Model Year Production

Year	Hardtop	Convertible	Fastback	Mach I	Grande
1965	501,965	101,945	77,079	–	–
1966	499,751	72,119	35,698	–	–
1967	356,271	44,808	71,042	–	–
1968	249,447	25,376	42,581	–	–
1969	128,458	14,746	61,980	72,458	22,182
1970	82,569	7,673	45,934	40,970	13,581
1971	65,696	6,121	23,956	36,499	17,406
1972	57,350	6,401	15,622	27,675	18,045
1973	51,480	11,853	10,820	35,440	25,674
Total	1,992,987	291,042	384,712	213,042	96,888

Shelby Mustang Model Year Production

	GT-350 coupe	GT-350 conv	GT-500 coupe	GT-500 conv	GT-500KR coupe	GT-500KR conv
1965	562	–	–	–	–	–
1966	2,378	**	–	–	–	–
1967	1,175	–	2,050	–	–	–
1968	1,253	404	1,140	402	933	318
1969	1,085	194	1,536	335	–	–
1970	[315]		[286]		–	–

** 6 convertibles built specially for friends of Carroll Shelby.
1970 bracketed figures are totals for each model; breakdowns by body type not available.

Engine Options by Model Year

Sixes

Cid	Bhp*	Standard	Optional
170	101	1964½	
200	115	1968-69	
200	120	1965-67, 1970	
250	155		1968-69
250	150		1970
250	145	1971	
250	98	1972	
250	99	1973	

V8s Cid	Bhp*	Standard	Optional		Cid	Bhp	Standard	Optional
260	164	1964½			351	330	1971(f)	
289	200	1965	1964½		390	320		1969
289	225		1964½-65		428	335		1969-70(c)
289	271		1964½-65		429	370		1971
302	210(e)	1971-73			429(d)	375		1969-70
302	220	1969-70(a)						
351	168(g)		1972-73					
351	200(g)		1972-73					
351	240		1971					
351	250		1969-70(b)					
351	275(g)		1972					
351	280		1971					
351	285		1971					

Notes:

(a) 290bhp standard Boss 302
(b) 250bhp 351 standard Mach I
(c) With and without Ram-Air
(d) Boss 429 only
(e) 95bhp nett 1972-73
(f) Boss 351 only
(g) Bhp is SAE nett
* Bhp is SAE gross unless noted otherwise

APPENDIX C

Comparative Mustang performance figures

Year	1965	1965	1965	1965	1965	1966	1967	1969	1969	1970 Boss	1972	1973
Model	H'top	Conv	Conv	Conv	GT 350	F'back	H'top	Mach 1	302	302	351 HO	Grande
CID	260	289	170	289	289	390	289	428	302	302	351	302
BHP	164	210	101	271	306	320	225	335	223	290	275	143
Transmission	auto	4-sp	auto	4-sp	4-sp	auto	4-sp	auto	auto	4-sp	4-sp	auto
Axle	3.00	3.00	3.50	4.11	3.89	3.00	3.00	3.91	2.79	3.91	3.91	2.79
Weight (lb)	2,847	3,053	2,791	3,103	2,850	3,414	2,980	3,607	3,500	3,415	3,604	3,260
Mean maximum (mph)	—	—	—	116	119	124	110	115	115	118	120	108
Acceleration (sec)												
0-30mph	4.8	3.6	4.9	3.6	2.6	2.6	3.6	2.1	3.6	—	2.6	3.7
0-40mph	—	—	—	4.6	3.4	4.2	5.3	3.0	5.4	3.2	3.6	5.5
0-50mph	8.8	6.9	9.2	6.2	4.6	5.6	7.4	4.4	7.4	—	5.0	7.7
0-60mph	11.2	8.9	12.5	8.2	6.5	7.3	9.7	5.7	9.6	6.0	6.6	10.4
0-80mph	—	—	—	13.6	10.3	11.7	16.1	9.5	17.2	10.0	10.8	18.3
0-100mph	48.0	27.5	—	21.6	17.0	18.9	27.0	14.3	32.9	15.2	16.4	36.7
¼-mile (sec)	18.8	17.0	20.0	16.0	14.9	15.2	17.4	14.3	—	14.6	15.1	17.7
¼-mile (mph)	78	85	74	87	95	91	84	100	—	93	96	79
Overall fuel consumption (mpg/US)	—	—	—	*12.8	7-14	10-14	14	—	*17	—	11-14	*15
Original test	5.64	5.64	5.64	10.64	5.65	11.66	3.67	11.68	9.69	2.70	3.72	11.72
Publication	R&T	R&T	R&T	Acar	C/D	C/D	R&T	C/D	CAR	C/D	C/D	Acar

(*Imperial gallons)

Publication reference: R&T – Road & Track; Acar – Autocar; C/D – Car and Driver; CAR – CAR Magazine

APPENDIX D

Things to look for: Mustang equipment guide

1965

RALLY-PAC: This was a combination rev counter and clock, available for all models, designed to mount atop the steering column just below and in front of the instrument panel. Collectors hoping to add Rally-Pacs to their cars should take into account several differences in this accessory. First, the unit designed for cars with the GT Equipment Group is different (mounts lower) than the standard version (which may be identified by a 'bridge' reading 'RALLY-PAC' between the two pods). This was done to accommodate the GT's 5-dial instrumentation. Second, internal mechanism of the rev counter differed for 6- and 8-cylinder models, and the appropriate Rally-Pac must be obtained. Finally, 271'H-P' Mustangs used an 8,000rpm calibration, while others used 6,000rpm. Rally-Pac can add from $250 to $400 to the value of the car.

GT EQUIPMENT GROUP: An option package introduced on the first anniversary of introduction (April 17, 1965). Included were the Special Handling Package, power front disc brakes, driving lamps mounted on an auxiliary inner grille bar, GT badges and special striping, bright metal bonnet moulding, 5-dial instrumentation, low-restriction dual exhausts with chrome-plated trumpet outlets through rear pan. GT equipment was available on the 225 and 271bhp V8s only when added at the factory, though some owners installed various parts or all of the package by retro-fit. The editors of *Mustang Monthly* note that factory GTs may be identified by their larger-size (disc brake) master cylinders with clip-on covers, 'DISC BRAKES' badge on brake pedal, steering gear ID tag containing letters 'HCC-AW' or 'HCC-AX' (denoting quick steering ratio) and the letter 'P' through 'V' in the warranty plate date code. This group adds 25-30% to the car's value.

PONY INTERIOR: Officially the Interior Decor Group, this was a mid-year option package distinguished by uniquely embossed vinyl seat backs with a panel containing a handsome octet of prancing ponies. Other components of this package were special door panels, padded sun visors, woodgrain-finished 5-dial instrument panel, simulated walnut grain steering wheel and walnut-grained door handles, bright metal trim on foot pedals, semi-carpeted kick panels with bright moulding, and red/white courtesy lights on the lower rear corner of each door. This package was availa-ble on all body styles; factory-installed packages are denoted by the letter 'B' following the body style number. Hence '63B' is a fastback with the option, while '65A' is a hardtop with the ordinary interior. This option adds $400-500 to the value of a closed model and $700-800 to the value of an open car.

OTHER DESIRABLE OPTIONS: Most power options improve the value of any Mustang, particularly the power top ($400-500), which is not often encountered on the convertibles. Air conditioning adds similar value, while the scarce AM radio with 8-track tape player adds about $300. The Accent Group (body side striping, rocker panel moulding, no rear-quarter bright trim; for hardtop and convertible only) adds about $100, while the Visibility Group (remote-control nearside mirror, day-night rear-view mirror, 2-speed wipers with screen wash) adds $200. Valuable individual options include dummy knock-off wheel covers ($100), simulated wire wheel covers ($300), styled steel wheels ($500), illuminated grille orna-ment ($100) and auxiliary clock mounted atop dashboard ($75). The Hand-ling Package alone ($150), front discs ($200) and various 4v V8s all add value, and the 271bhp engine can alone add 50%. The between-seats con-sole (full-length normal, short-length when air conditioning fitted) adds $100-150, while the wood-grained steering wheel alone is worth $150-200 extra.

1966

The same comments apply to the 1966 model as to the 1965. All Mustangs now adopted the handsome 5-dial instrumentation, but the Interior Decor Package continued to include walnut graining around the gauges and matching finish on the glovebox. The low-mount Rally-Pac was now the only type used. The various wheel options remained available, though the styled steel wheels were redesigned to use more matt black finish and less chromium plate. The GT Group remained available on 225 and 271bhp models and now included a special fuel cap with 'GT' identification. As in 1965, rear overriders were deleted from GT models.

SPRINT 200: A specially equipped Mustang six, this desirable sub-model came with striping, chrome-plated air cleaner, 'SPRINT' decal on engine, wire-type wheel covers, full centre console, padded dash and sun visors, outside rear-view mirror, seat belts, reversing lamps, emergency flasher, screen wash and electric wipers, but no performance or handling improvements. The Sprint option adds about 25% to the value of a Mustang Six.

1967

GT EQUIPMENT GROUP: Expanded this year to be available for any V8 including automatic transmission models (which then received special 'GTA' badge on front wings), and also including F70 x 14 Wide-Oval whitewall tyres. The low-restriction dual exhaust system with trumpet outlets was fitted only to 4v GTs; the GT-identified petrol cap was of the pop-open variety when the Exterior Decor Group was specified. Value comments as per 1965.

REV COUNTER: In lieu of the Rally-Pac, Ford now offered an optional rev-counter designed to fit the large right-hand gauge pod ordinarily filled by the oil/amps gauges. These functions were unfortunately consigned to warning lights, built into the lower quadrant of the rev-counter's face. As before, 271bhp 289s received an 8,000rpm unit, others 6,000rpm. Also included in the tachometer option was a special speedometer with a trip odometer. This option adds $100-200 to the car's value.

COMPETITION HANDLING SUSPENSION: A 'second stage' handling package, mainly for racing and serious rallying, this option included extra stiff springs front and rear, adjustable shock absorbers, oversize anti-roll bars, extra-quick steering with 16:1 ratio, Limited-slip differential with a minimum ratio of 3.25:1 and 15 x 6in wheels with wire wheel covers; was available only with the GT Equipment Group. Mustang enthusiasts advise the author that this system adds $400-500 to the value of a car, but it may be something one can do without for ordinary motoring. Mustangs so fitted are hard-riding and best suited to the drag strip; undoubtedly, they were also the best handling models offered by the factory thus far.

INTERIOR DECOR GROUP: Similar to previous versions, but lacking the 'pony' seatback motif, this package included moulded door trim panels with integral armrests, lower inside door panel grille work housing red/white courtesy lights, roof console on closed models, bright pedal trim, brushed aluminium instrument panel/glovebox door, electric clock and vinyl-covered shifter handle on automatics. This group adds about $300 to the car's value.

INDY PACESETTER SPECIAL: A curious mid-year package (Mustang did **not** pace the 1967 Indy 500), this car offered special dual striping running full-length below the beltline on the hardtop model only. Limited production gives it a certain desirability. Adds 10-15% to car's value.

CONVENIENCE CONTROL PANEL: A set of four red warning lights mounted in a walnut-grained panel fitted to the centre of the dashboard (or console on cars with air conditioning). The warning lights notified the driver of parking brake on, door ajar, seat belts unhooked or low fuel (under 4 US gallons). Adds $100-150 to car's value.

1968

SPORTS TRIM GROUP: A new package consisting of wood-grained instrument panel, bright wheel lip mouldings, knit-style seat inserts (closed cars), duotoned bonnet with matt black twin stripes. On V8s, this group also included 'Argent' painted styled steel wheels and E70 x 14 Wide-Oval whitewalls tyres. The louvred bonnet option was mandatory with this group. Adds $300-350 to car's value.

GT EQUIPMENT GROUP: Again available only with 4v V8s, including GT emblem on front wings, GT-emblazoned pop-open fuel cap, low-restriction dual exhaust with four outlets (2 groups of 2), driving or fog lamps (their effectiveness in either application is ever debated by collectors) without the extra grille bar, new striping (straight back from far forward, down behind the doors, straight forward to taper out at mid-door), chrome-styled steel wheels with GT badging, F70 x 14 Wide-Oval whitewall tyres, H-D suspension and chrome-plated components for 390/427 engines when fitted. Previous GT rocker panel striping was also available. An additional Reflective Group could be had, providing reflective striping and reflective 'Argent' paint on styled wheels. Adds 25-30% to car's value.

INTERIOR DECOR GROUP: Most easily identified by twin bright buttons in each seatback, this package again included the usual touches, updated where necessary. The upper door panel insert used vertically pleated vinyl fitted with a pull strap, and was divided from the lower panel by a wood-grained strip. Also included were a wood-grained steering wheel and, on closed models, a roof console carrying twin map lights. Adds $300 to car's value.

SPRINT: Available on sixes and V8s in hardtop body only, this package included GT stripes, pop-open fuel cap, 'SPRINT' identification and full wheel covers. With V8 engines, Wide-Oval tyres, styled steel wheels and fog/driving lamps were added. Adds 10% to car's value.

INDIVIDUAL AND DEALER-INSTALLED OPTIONS: See 1965 comments.

COBRA JET: Special 428-powered fastback introduced April 1, 1968, with GT striping, styled steel wheels and heavy-duty suspension added to the following special features: lower shock tower bracing, functional bonnet scoop, H-D rear axle with staggered shocks when 4-speed fitted, power front disc brakes, 8,000rpm tachometer (standard on 4-speeds, optional with automatic). The CJ was immediately identifiable by a wide matt black stripe running down the bonnet, encompassing the scoop. Extremely scarce, a Cobra Jet can be worth from 75 to 100% more than a comparable-condition standard V8 fastback.

CALIFORNIA SPECIAL: Perhaps unfortunately named (we all have our own interpretation of those words), the CS was a dealer offering in Southern California; it came as a base six-cylinder hardtop, but was usually found with the various V8s. Fittings were the bolt-on variety, but many added to its driveability. There were Lucas (occasionally Marchal) driving lamps set into a blacked-out grille without the usual galloping pony, a glassfibre boot lid/spoiler and Shelby-style tail panel, body side striping between the wheel wells ending in a dummy scoop emblazoned 'GT/CS', a louvred bonnet (standard Ford option) with special hold-down twist-locks, and considerable identifying script: 'California Special' on the rear wings, 'Mustang' on the lower front quarters and the spoiler. Adds 50% to value of comparable standard hardtop.

HIGH COUNTRY SPECIAL: Another dealer concoction, this time produced by the Colorado agencies, virtually identical to the California Special, but lacking the chrome rear wing script and replacing the side scoop lettering with an attractive triangular badge. Even more limited than the CS, this is a highly desirable variation that adds 75% to the value of an ordinary hardtop.

1969
GT EQUIPMENT GROUP: Now in its last year, this group was available in all body styles fitted with 351, 390 or 428 V8. It consisted of a plain lower body side racing stripe, non-functional bonnet scoop (functional when CJ Ram-Air 428 was installed – in this guise it was the famous 'Shaker' scoop), pin-style bonnet hold-down pins, styled steel wheels, E70 x 14 whitewall tyres, H-D suspension, pop-open 'GT' fuel-filler cap and – when 4v V8s were ordered – low-restriction dual exhaust. Adds 25-30% to car's value.

HIGH-BACK BUCKET SEATS: A first-time option, available with all interiors and all models. Useful safety feature, but not significant in collector value.

CONSOLE: Redesigned this year, blending with its interior, with raised armrest covering auxiliary glove compartment towards the rear. The 1969 console contains seat belts latches, ashtray and cigar lighter. Colour is black with standard interior, colour-keyed with woodgraining when fitted to special interiors. Adds $100-150 to car's value.

DELUXE INTERIOR DECOR GROUP: Now available on closed models only, the 1969 package consisted of wood-grained dash and door panel inserts, dark grey (instead of black) instrument faces with altered numeration on speedometer, specially upholstered seats with quilted pattern in top seat back. On Deluxe models, this was titled the INTERIOR DECOR GROUP and was also available on convertibles. Wood-graining and clock were part of Deluxe IDG only. Adds $150 to car value.

INDIVIDUAL AND DEALER INSTALLED OPTIONS continued to be offered

in profusion, and comments under 1965 entry still apply. Dollar values when given are, however, increasingly low, as overall value of basic models begins to move downward, starting with 1967.

POWER VENTILATION SYSTEM: New option and a low-cost alternative to air conditioning, using heater-blown cool air ducted through centre-dashboard outlets. A useful option if you find it, the system adds about $50 to the car's value. Cars so fitted have a power vent position on the heater control panel.

MUSTANG 'E' SPORTSROOF: Of limited collector significance, probably, but it may be encountered in the field. This was an Economy package including six-cylinder engine, lower numerical rear axle ratio and automatic transmission with economy torque converter. Production figures are unknown, but probably did not exceed several thousand units.

1970
FLAIR DECOR GROUP: The sole interior option that year, offered for standard models in all body styles, it included high-back bucket seats with knit-type vinyl inserts or 'Blazer Stripe' inserts as the customer preferred, wood-grained panels on dash and door trim, dark grey instrument facings with altered speedometer markings, deluxe two-spoke steering wheel, twin racing rear-view mirrors colour-keyed to exterior paint (remote control for driver's mirror), bright trim on rocker panels and wheel lip mouldings unless F60 x 15 tyres fitted. Adds $300 to car's value.

VINYL ROOF OPTIONS: Although these had been around for some time, 1970 was unique in offering a 'Western' pattern, in which a fancy tooled-style embossed vinyl strip carried around the lower edge of the vinyl for the full perimeter of the greenhouse. A houndstooth-pattern vinyl roof was also offered for the basic hardtop or Grande. Either of these variations adds about $100-150.

TACHOMETER: Available with V8 models only, the rev-counter again replaced the temp/fuel gauges in the large right-hand instrument pod. These moved left and right into the smaller openings, but they also displaced the standard oil/amps gauges, which again were rendered into warning lights. The package included a trip odometer speedometer and a brake system warning light. Adds $100 to a car's value.

DRAG PACK: Offered as a 428 V8 option, this package included Traction-Lok differential with 3.91:1 final-drive ratio or the Detroit-Locker No-Spin differential with 4.30:1 ratio, plus engine oil cooler, modified flywheel/crankshaft/damper and cap-screw connecting rods. It adds at least $500 to a car's value.

COMPETITION SUSPENSION: As in the past, this included extra H-D springs and shocks, stiff rollbars front and rear, and was available with the

4v 351 and 428 V8s with automatic. It could also be ordered for the 4-speed 4v 428, in which case it included staggered rear shocks. Adds $300-400 to car's value.

GRABBER: A special SportsRoof trim package offered in mid-year 1970, the Grabber included reflective striping and special flat hub caps with matching trim rings on 14in wheels. The Boss 302/351 Grabber used different striping, extending downwards from the forward part of the door and then back to the rear wheel wells, carrying a '302' or '351' nomenclature and not reflectorized. Adds 10% to SportsRoof models, 15-20% to Boss models.

1971
CONVENIENCE GROUP: A typical Detroit option, this package provided courtesy lamps in the boot, under the bonnet and in the glovebox, plus a central map lamp, a glove compartment lock, a warning buzzer for headlamps on, an automatic seat back release, a parking brake warning light and under-dash courtesy lamps (standard on convertibles). Adds $100-150 to car value.

INSTRUMENTATION GROUP: A more thorough juggling of instruments to provide more information to the driver than before, this option now provided individual oil pressure, alternator and temperature gauges at the centre of the dashboard, mounted in a special housing which replaced the standard 'galloping pony' emblem, plus the usual rev-counter (8,000rpm standard), fitted in the left-hand instrument panel pod. The trip odometer was again fitted to speedometers in this application. The group was standard on Boss 351s, optional on other models except 250cid 6-cyls. Adds $200 to car value.

POWER SIDE WINDOWS: A first-time option in 1971, this package also included a lock-out switch on the driver's master panel. SportsRoof rear windows, which were not ordinarily fully retractable, went down all the way with this option, whose scarcity adds about $250 to car value.

OTHER: The usual decor group, console, seat variations and individual options were available and previous comments continue to apply.

SPORTS HARDTOP: A Spring 1971 appearance package including honeycomb grillework, colour-keyed bumper, scoop-type bonnet, lower body side contrasting paint matched by Boss 351 body side striping. Adds 10% to value.

1972
Retrenchment and contraction of the long Mustang option list was occurring as the hotter varieties began to disappear and the ponycar market itself contracted. The Interior Decor Group of 1971 was deleted, while convertible interiors at least were much improved as standard, with knit-style vinyl seat inserts and moulded door panels with wood-grain trim.

EXTERIOR DECOR GROUP: A new option which provided lower body side special paint with chrome moulding, unique honeycomb grille containing 'Sportslamps', colour-keyed bonnet/wing mouldings and front bumper, brushed aluminium hub caps. Offered for standard hardtops and convertibles, it adds 10% to car value.

DUAL RAM INDUCTION: Functional Ram-Air bonnet for V8 models, restricted to 2v 351 V8s at mid-year; included duotone paint, Ram-Air engine decals and twist-lock bonnet hold-down pins. Uncommon, this adds $300 to car value.

SPRINT PACKAGE: Offered in two forms from February 1972, on red, white and blue-trimmed closed models. Type A: white body; red and blue bonnet stripes, lower body paint and rear pan; 'USA' emblem on rear wings; twin colour-keyed racing-type rear-view mirrors; brushed aluminium hub caps; E70 x 14 whitewalls tyres; white vinyl interior with blue Lambeth cloth seat inserts and special carpeting; Exterior Decor Group. Type B: As above, but with Magnum 500 wheels and F60 x 15 tyres. Type A adds 15%, Type B 20% to car value. (Similarly equipped Pintos and Mavericks were also sold at the same time.)

1973
As per 1972, and earlier comments for individual options.

LEATHER WRAPPED STEERING WHEEL: Available on 2-spoke wheels, adds $50 to car value.

APPENDIX E

Relative Mustang values in 1983

Mustang values, which arose astonishingly between 1975 and 1980, seemed to level off during the recession years of the early 'Eighties, but as the economy of Western nations revives, they may be in for further increases. Certainly, no desirable model will ever be worth less than it is today, and the supply of the 'most-desirable' model years, 1965-66, has to taper off sometime. Some of the following values are quoted with permission from *The Complete Book of Collectable Cars 1940-1980* by the author and Graham Robson, courtesy of the publishers, Publications International Inc, Skokie, Illinois. They are meant as guidelines, not as hard-and-fast rules; when evaluating any Mustang the enthusiast should take into account the various desirable extras or sub-models listed in Appendix D, as well as other price guides readily available. The most authoritative of these is the *Mustang Value Guide,* published annually by the editors of *Mustang Monthly* magazine.

The three categories used here are: 'Restorable' (all those, possibly not running, in need of considerable work, but not a 'basket-case' or a totally rusted out example); 'Good' (completely driveable, either original or an older restoration, needing some obvious mechanical and cosmetic work, possibly a repaint, rechroming and some interior work, but not a whole new interior, new engine or complete body restoration); 'Excellent' (fine original or restored condition, 85% perfect or better, with all components functioning, nothing missing, or nothing of signficance required). We again emphasize that these are general, ballpark price ranges; Mustangs will be found between, above and below the figures quoted, and there will be instances of extreme cases both ways. A year or so ago a Mustang was reported sold at auction at $20,000, proof as ever that Barnum was right.

1965-66
Basic hardtop: restorable $500-900, good $1,250-2,500, excellent $2,500-4,000. Add 50% for convertible, 25% for fastback, 20% for HO 271bhp, 30% for GT Equipment Package, and particularly see also Appendix D. Deduct 15% for 6-cylinder engine, 10%-25% for non-factory modifications. Five-year projections: V8s +50%, Sixes +25%.

1967-68
Basic hardtop: restorable $400-800, good $1,000-2,000, excellent $2,200-3,500. Add 50% for convertible, 25% for fastback, 15-20% for HO 289 or big-block V8s, 25-30% for GT Equipment Package. Deduct 15% for 6-cylinder engine, 10-25% for non-factory modifications. Five-year projection: +20%.

1969-70
Basic hardtop: restorable $400-800, good $800-1,700, excellent $1,500-3,000. Add 30% for convertible, 15% for fastback, 15-20% for performance V8, 30% for 1969 GT Equipment. Deduct 10% for 6-cylinder engine. Boss 302: restorable $1,000-2,000, good $2,000-3,500, excellent $3,500-6,000. Boss 429: restorable $1,500-2,500, good $2,500-4,500, excellent $4,500-7,000. Mach I: restorable $750-1,250, good $1,250-2,500, excellent $2,500-3,500. Five-year projection: Boss/Mach I +35%, others +20%.

1971-73
Closed models: restorable $300-700, good $700-1,500, excellent $1,500-2,800. Convertibles: restorable $500-1,200, good $1,200-2,000, excellent $2,200-3,500. Add 20% for HO V8, add 20% for 4-speed, deduct 20% for 6-cylinder engine. Five-year projection: Mach I +20%, others even.

Shelby Mustangs
There is a great deal of controversy about the values of early Shelbys. Rick Kopec, of the Shelby American Automobile Club, wrote to the author: 'It is unheard of for any Shelby but the most wrecked or rotted out to be sold for anything less than around $4,000. They're worth more than that in parts alone, if the parts are still with the car. Likewise, we're seeing the top cars being advertised for upwards of $12,000 to $15,000. But these are usually asking prices, and the cars are usually sold for a figure under that.' The values shown are, we feel, reasonable, considering the volatility of the Shelby market, but as with any collector's item, value does not always mean the same to different people, nor does it respond to logical calculation. I would strongly urge membership in SAAC, followed by careful observation of their articles and adverts, before beginning to shop for a GT-350 or GT-500.

1965-66
GT-350: restorable $4,000-5,500, good $6,000-8,000, excellent $9,000-11,000. Deduct $1,000 if 1966 model. Five-year projection: +25%.

1967

GT-350: restorable $3,000-4,500, good $5,000-7,000, excellent $8,000-10,000. GT-500: restorable $3,000-5,000, good $5,000-7,500, excellent $8,500-10,000. Five-year projection: GT-350 +35%, GT-500 +50%.

1968

GT-350: restorable $3,000-$4,000, good $4,000-6,000, excellent $6,000-

8,000. GT-500 hardtop: restorable $3,500-4,500, good $4,500-6,500, excellent $7,500-9,000. Convertibles: add 25-35%. GT-500KR hardtop: restorable $5,000-6,000, good $7,000-9,000, excellent $9,000-11,000. GT500KR convertible: add 35%. Five-year projection: +50%, 500KR +75%.

English pound sterling at time of publication was worth US $1.50. For sterling price divide by 1.5. These prices apply mainly to the USA market.

APPENDIX F

VIN ordinaire: Decoding the serial number

You call it 'serial' or 'commission' number, but Ford calls it 'VIN' – Vehicle Identification Number. With Mustangs, it's important beyond its obvious necessity for registration purposes. It tells you what kind of a Mustang you have – or are about to make an offer for. Ergo, a fundamental understanding of this perfectly ordinary coding system is important.

The VIN will be found in various places on various year Mustangs. The place-of-record is on the upper top flange of the left front fender (wing) apron (1965-67), on the passenger side instrument panel close under the windscreen (1968), or on the driver-side instrument panel under the screen (1969-73). The 1968-73 VIN is stamped on a small aluminium plate riveted to dashboard, and is readily visible from outside the car looking in. (VIN also appears on a warranty plate riveted to the rear inside edge of the driver's door through to 1969 or affixed to an owner's card from 1970, as well as on the Vehicle Certification Label for Federal safety standards. But the place-of-record is one of the aforementioned locations.)

To define meanings, let us take a typical VIN:

5 F 0 8 A 1 2 3 4 5 6

5	F	0 8	A	1 2 3 4 5 6
Model year (last digit)	Assembly plant	Body type	Engine type	Consecutive unit number

MODEL YEAR: 1965 through to 1963.

ASSEMBLY PLANT: F = Dearborn, Michigan: R = San Jose, California; T = Metuchen, New Jersey.

BODY TYPE CODE: Eight different digits may be encountered; the Boss models are not, however, distinguished by this code.

01 = 1967-73 hardtop
02 = 1967-73 fastback or SportsRoof
03 = 1967-73 convertible
04 = 1970-73 Grande
05 = 1970-73 Mach I
06 = not assigned
07 = 1965-66 hardtop
08 = 1965-66 convertible
09 = 1965-66 fastback

ENGINE TYPE CODE: With the variation possible on Mustangs, this is one of the most important identifying items on the car and should definitely be verified against the engine actually installed. Code meanings are as follows:

A = 4v 289cid V8, 1965-67
C = 2v 289cid V8, 1965-68; Cobra-Jet (CJ/SCJ) 429cid V8, 1971
D = 4v 289cid low-compression V8, early 1965 only
F = 2v 260cid V8, 1965; 2v 302cid V8, 1968-73
G = 4v Boss 302cid V8, 1969-70
H = 2v 351cid V8, 1969-73 (with Ram-Air 1972-73)
J = 4v 302cid V8, 1968; Cobra-Jet (CJ/SCJ) 429cid Ram-Air V8, 1971
K = 4v Hi-Performance 289cid (271bhp) V8, 1965-67
L = 1v 250cid six, 1969-73
M = 4v 351cid V8, 1969-71

Q = 4v 428cid V8, 1969-70; 4v 351cid V8, 1971-73 (with Ram-Air 1971)
R = 4v 428cid Ram-Air V8, 1968-70; 4v Boss 351 V8, 1971; 4v HO V8, 1972 (Cobra Jet & Shelby GT-500KR)
S = 4v 390cid V8, 1967-69; also 4v 428cid Shelby, 1968
T = 1v 200cid six, 1965-70
U = 1v 170cid six, early 1965
W = 4v 427cid V8, 1968
X = 2v 390cid V8, 1968-69
Y = 2v 390cid V8, 1968-69
Z = 4v Boss 429cid V8, 1969-70
2 = 4v 289cid V8, 1967; Shelby 289cid V8, 1968
4 = 8v 428cid Shelby V8, 1967 GT-500

SHELBY MUSTANGS: From 1965 to 1967, Shelbys have an auxiliary serial number riveted on top of the VIN. In 1968, while the Ford VIN was relocated to the passenger side of the instrument panel, the Shelby number remained on the inner fender (wing) left-hand panel as before. For 1969-70, no additional Shelby numeration appears on the VIN plate or elsewhere, but genuine Shelbys (counterfeits are now something to watch for) all have a plate reading 'SHELBY AUTOMOTIVE' riveted beneath the Warranty Plate. (Since 1970 Shelbys were simply reserialed 1969 models, they did not change from Warranty Plate to Federal Certification Plate, as did 1970 production Mustangs.) If there is any doubt as to the authenticity of any car represented as a Shelby, the prospective purchaser should apply to the Shelby American Automobile Club for expertise and assistance.

BODY STYLE CODES: The Warranty Plate (1965-69) or Certification Label (1970-73) contains a useful code under the heading 'BODY', which should be referred to when determining the original interior fitted by the factory. Code meanings are as follows:

63A = std interior, bucket-seat fastback, 1965-68, SportsRoof 1969-70
63B = luxury interior, bucket-seat fastback, 1965-68 SportsRoof 1969-70
63C = standard interior, bench seat fastback, 1968; Mach I, 1969-70
63D = luxury interior, bench seat fastback, 1968; standard interior, bucket-seat SportsRoof 1971-73
63R = Mach I, 1971-73
65A = standard interior, bucket-seat hardtop, 1965-70
65B = luxury interior, bucket-seat hardtop, 1965-70
65C = standard interior, bench seat hardtop, 1965-69
65D = luxury interior, bench seat hardtop, 1968-69; standard interior, bucket-seat hardtop, 1971-73
65E = Grande, 1969-70
65F = Grande, 1971-73
76A = standard interior, bucket-seat convertible, 1965-70
76B = luxury interior, bucket-seat convertible, 1965-70
76C = standard interior, bench seat convertible, 1965-67
76D = standard interior, bucket-seat convertible, 1971-73

APPENDIX G

Further reading: The best books

Mustang books are legion, and the 1965-73 generation is probably the best documented single model since the Ford Model T. A number of books are particularly helpful to collectors, and I list them in the order in which I would personally want to acquire them, were I able to order only one at a time. Most books may be obtained from the publishers or from Connoisseur Carbooks, 28 & 32 Devonshire Road, Chiswick, London W4 2HD, England, or Classic Motorbooks, PO Box 2 Osceola, Wisconsin 54020, USA.

MUSTANG RECOGNITION GUIDE, 1964½ THRU 1973, by the Editors of *Mustang Monthly*, PO Drawer 6320, Lakeland, Florida 33803, 226 pages, $16.95

This book is not only beautifully produced with a surfeit of four-colour illustration; it is also the most authoritative spotter's guide to virtually every Mustang model, performance option, accessory and dealer special built through to 1973. Each model year is exhaustively described from exterior and interior, through wheels and tyres, power teams, suspension, specs and options. Essential not only for the shopper, but for the restorer intent on insuring that this car is absolutely 'factory-stock'. Highly recommended.

SHELBY AMERICAN GUIDE, by Rick Kopec, Shelby-American Automobile Club, 22 Olmstead Road, West Redding, Connecticut 06896, 96 pages, $10.95.

Without a doubt the most accurate and comprehensive guide to the many intricate alleyways explored by Shelby American during the golden years of the great fire-breathing GT-350/500s. Expertly researched by a top Shelby watcher with the active assistance of Shelby American people, profusely illustrated, and just about indispensible for the prospective Shelby owner.

MUSTANG ENCYCLOPEDIA, by the Editors of Consumer Guide, 3841 West Oakton, Stokie, Illinois 60076, 228 pages, $14.95.

The outstanding feature of this bargain-priced hardback is its well illustrated step-by-step restoration of an early fastback. Unfortunately the car was a Six, and the more complicated details of V8 restoration are necessarily left out. Some reviewers have said it's too basic ('To get at the front

pan you must first remove the bumper'), but for anyone who is about to tackle Mustang bodywork and interior reconstruction, it's the clearest guide on the market. Also included is a huge list of Mustang spares dealers, clubs, publications and other specialists, which is very comprehensive, and a detailed history of the marque. There are sections on driving impressions, specifications, competition and collecting, plus 400 illustrations and 60 colour plates. Had anybody other than Consumer Guide published it, it would have cost $40.00.

HOW TO RESTORE YOUR MUSTANG, by Larry Dobbs, *Mustang Monthly*, PO Drawer 6320, Lakeland, Florida 33803, 156 pages, $14.95.

Another step-by-step guide to the home restorer that anyone contemplating such a task must have before he begins work. Confining himself to 1965-68 models, the author begins with 'Selection and Planning' and works his way through the entire process down to the final details. Softbound with 400 illustrations and seven colour plates. Useful and professionally done.

MUSTANG: THE COMPLETE HISTORY, by Gary L. Witzenburg, *Automobile Quarterly*, PO Box 348, Kutztown, Pennsylvania 19530, 204 pages, $29.95.

Expensive, but also thorough, this is the standard history of Mustang from the beginning through to 1979, backed by research and interviews with the people who designed and built it, those who raced it, and the salesmen who flogged it. Photographs illustrate all phases of design including the 1974 Mustang II and the current generation, as well as production cars, competition, etc. Includes 24 pages in colour.

THE OFFICIAL MUSTANG BLACK BOOK, by the Editors of *Mustang Monthly*, PO Drawer 6320, Lakeland, Florida 33803, 42 pages, $4.95.

An almost incredibly detailed examination of Mustang values, cranking into the formula an exact value for nearly every major accessory and option group. The problem here is that it is very difficult to establish hard and fast prices down to such a fine line, because collector Mustangs don't change hands nearly as frequently as ordinary used cars, and the perceived value of an item necessarily varies from person to person. Even so, a very useful basic guide which will tell you what to look for and approximately what it's worth when you find it.

SHELBY BUYERS GUIDE, by Rick Kopec, Shelby-American Automobile Club, 22 Olmstead Road, West Redding, Connecticut 06896, 80 pages, $10.95.

The Shelby version of the above, again written by the knowledgeable Kopec, designed to help the buyer identify the full range of Shelbys in all their complexity, complete with factory specifications and the latest production figures. Good value, well presented.

MUSTANG BOSS 302, by Donald Farr, *Mustang Monthly,* PO Drawer 6320, Lakeland, Florida 33803, 114 pages, $12.95.

An in-depth study of Ford's answer to the Z/28 Camaro, on both the street and the Trans-Am track. The author takes you back to where it all started and records facts as told by the men who conceived, designed and developed the Boss 302. A valuable guide to identifying a genuine car, helpful tips on buying one, and containing hundreds of photographs and drawings including many in colour.

ILLUSTRATED HIGH-PERFORMANCE MUSTANG BUYER'S GUIDE, by Peter C. Sessler, Motorbooks International Publishers & Wholesalers Inc., PO Box 2, Osceola, Wisconsin 54020, 148 pages, $13.95.

GT, Mach I, Boss and Shelby Mustangs described in separate chapters with 187 supporting pictures to aid identification. Lots of useful tabular data concerning performance, equipment, clubs, parts and service.

APPENDIX H

Fellowship: The Mustang car clubs

MUSTANG CLUB OF AMERICA
PO Box 447, Lithonia, Georgia 30058
Founded 1976, 4,000 members, 57 chapters.
Specializes in 1965-73 models.
Subscription/dues, $20 per year.

MUSTANG OWNERS CLUB
2829 Cagua Drive NE, Albuquerque, New Mexico 87110
Founded 1975, 750 members.
Welcomes all Mustang owners and enthusiasts.
Subscription/dues, $10 per year.

SHELBY AMERICAN AUTOMOBILE CLUB
22 Olmstead Road, West Redding, Connecticut 06896
Founded 1975, 6,500 members, numerous chapters.
Welcomes Shelby Mustangs, Cobras, GT40s, Sunbeam Tigers.
Publishes **The Shelby American** five times per year.
Subscription/dues, $27.50 per year.

SHELBY OWNERS OF AMERICA
2851 South Mead, Wichita, Kansas 67216
Founded 1976, 400 members.
Welcomes Shelby and Boss Mustangs.
Subscription/dues, $15 individual, $17.50 per couple.

BOSS MUSTANG OWNERS ASSOCIATION
PO Box 1085, La Mirada, California 90637
Founded 1979, 400 members.
Open to all owners of Boss 302, 351 and 429 Mustangs.
Subscription/dues, $8 per year.

INDEPENDENT REGIONAL CLUBS:
Mustang & Classic Ford Club of New England, PO Box 963, North Attleboro, Massachusetts 02761. (Founded 1980, 200 members, subs $15, bimonthly magazine.)

Mustang Car Club of New England, PO Box 1554, Woonsocket, Rhode Island 02895. (Founded 1978, 300 members, subs $15, Mustang owners only, monthly newsletter.)

Mustang Club of Southern California, 15168 Ashwood Lane, Chino, California 91710. (Founded 1979, 175 members, bimonthly newsletter, subs $12.)

Mustang Owners Club of California, PO Box 7321, Van Nuys, California 91409. (Founded 1977, 800 members, welcomes 1965-73 models, two chapters, subs $18.)

National Capital Region Mustang Club, 9397 Shouse Drive, Vienna, Virginia 22180. (Founded 1979, 200 members, bimonthly newsletter, subs $9.)